Patrick Geddes: The French Connection

The Contributors

DR ELIZABETH CUMMING publishes internationally on Scottish art and design since 1850. An Honorary Senior Research Fellow at the University of Glasgow, she was Canterbury Visiting Fellow in the School of Fine Arts, University of Canterbury, New Zealand in 2003.

DR FRANCES FOWLE is Curator and Leverhulme Research Fellow at the National Gallery of Scotland and Honorary Fellow in History of Art at the University of Edinburgh. She has published widely on Scottish collecting and 19th-century French and Scottish art.

MURDO MACDONALD is Professor of History of Scottish Art at the University of Dundee. He has a long-standing interest in Patrick Geddes and is currently working on a book about Geddes and cultural revivals. He is author of *Scottish Art* (2000).

SIÂN REYNOLDS is Professor Emeritus of French at the University of Stirling. She has published extensively on French and Scottish history, including *France Between the Wars: Gender and Politics* (1996). She is currently researching a book on Paris and Edinburgh in the belle époque.

BELINDA THOMSON, who chaired the Geddes exhibition committee, is Honorary Fellow in History of Art at the University of Edinburgh. She publishes widely on late 19th-century French art, specialising in Gauguin and the Nabi group. She is the author of monographs on *Gauguin* (1987, 2001) and *Vuillard* (1988).

Patrick Geddes:
The French Connection

EDITED BY FRANCES FOWLE
AND BELINDA THOMSON

Published by

White Cockade Publishing
71 Lonsdale Road
Oxford OX2 7ES
Tel. 01865 510411
www.whitecockade.co.uk

in association with
The Scottish Society for Art History

British Library Cataloguing-in-Publication Data
A catalogue record for this book is available from the British Library.

ISBN 1 873487 11 8 paperback

Editing and design by Perilla Kinchin

Printed and bound in Great Britain by The Alden Press Ltd, Oxford

Frontispiece: Patrick Geddes photographed by Eirwyn MacGillivray in the dining
room of Ramsay Garden, 1912. The thistle and *fleur de lys* design on the title
page is based on the fireplace. © National Library of Scotland.

Contents

Foreword

Anyone who tries to pigeonhole the extraordinary Patrick Geddes, fails. His interests and activities were legion. Over the last hundred years, many distinguished writers and academics have tried to define Geddes. They all agree on one thing: he defies categorisation. He was the ultimate polymath, an interdisciplinary thinker and action man in a multiplicity of vibrant areas of activity.

I live and write in a property renovated by Geddes and decorated under his direction. For several years this very room served as a forum for Geddes's annual Summer Meetings, international events which offer a remarkable foretaste of our own Edinburgh Festival. I have looked out on several major cities, and city landscapes, recreated or regenerated by him. I have read letters from his artist friend and colleague – my godfather, John Duncan – to my own father, following a visit they made to France together, trying to define the kernel of Geddes, and have listened to lectures, and read much that has been seeded by his intellect.

Botanist, sociologist, educationalist, 'Father of Modern Town Planning', this purveyor of the concept of 'synthesis' between disciplines, was friend and inspiration to many in France, from the highest members of the artistic, political, social, and scientific, establishment of the Third Republic, to some of the most notorious international anarchists of that dangerous age. In that other lovely city, Montpellier, for example, where he lived for some considerable time, and where he died, they benefited greatly from his skills. That city's fathers listened and learned from his arguments about not allowing traffic to dominate our lives, making it the civilised, pedestrianised place it is today. In this and other ways, he made his mark on France, but through his network of contacts, he and his ideas crossed many other frontiers as well, changing attitudes as far afield as Palestine and India.

Patrick Geddes's 'conservative surgery' as he called it, preserved from decay much of what the Old Town of Edinburgh is today. Oh that he had been around half a century later, when the City and the University between them vandalised so much of central Edinburgh. How he would shudder today to see the way so many of his heroic efforts to restore the very heart of Edinburgh have fallen into a deplorable and squalid state once more. Maybe the current exhibition and other events being held in 2004 to celebrate the 150th anniversary of his birth will waken the consciences of this city once more.

MICHAEL SHEA

Preface and Acknowledgements

Patrick Geddes was a distinguished Scot whose ideas were ahead of his time and whose impact was felt far beyond his native shores. One hundred and fifty years after his birth his thinking continues to have relevance. Yet his reputation has veered – and if for some he is an inspirational figure, others have dismissed him as an eccentric crank. Although he famously built outlook towers from which to survey the world Geddes was no ivory tower scholar but a man of action. His thinking machines, distilling into visual schemata the complex motivations of human life, have lasting value. As a trained botanist and biologist, Geddes was a pioneering 'green' campaigner. Passionate about ecology – his famous dictum being 'by leaves we live' – he foresaw the problems that indiscriminate deforestation would cause in the future. Accepting that modern society would be increasingly urbanised he focused his thinking on how to make cities culturally rich and sustainable co-operative environments. Not a wealthy man himself, he was adept at finding sponsors, sweeping up businessmen as well as young artists and architects in his project to rejuvenate Edinburgh's Old Town. He was regarded with suspicion in certain quarters of Edinburgh because of his connections with anarchist politics. His vision for university education included its extension to women and to working men, a de-emphasis on examinations and bureaucracy and a promotion of field work and international academic exchange.

A great traveller, Geddes considered that learning other languages and absorbing other cultures was essential for the modern scholar, the best way of promoting international understanding and peace. Underlying many of his ideas and aspirations lay French experiences and French contacts. He argued that the modern world ignored the model of France at its peril. France, for Geddes, had her priorities right. There, art was central to life, the highest artistic standards being brought to the most mundane aspects of daily living: witness her cuisine or the exquisite design of her coinage. As a culmination of several efforts at rapprochement, Geddes gave concrete expression to his commitment to France in Paris in 1900 and in Montpellier, where he established the Scots College and the Indian College alongside it.

Around 1890, Geddes envisaged a cultural renaissance in Edinburgh as a complement to the urban renewal work he had undertaken in the Old Town. This took various forms, which are discussed in the essays: Summer Meetings of Art and Science, the publication of *The Evergreen* and the commissioning of the complex of buildings that makes up Ramsay Lodge and Ramsay Garden. Running through all of these cultural manifestations there was a French thread, be it in terms of content, the personalities involved, the ideas presented or the styles favoured. Emblematic of his wish to revive

Scottish cultural links with France was Geddes's linking of the *fleur de lys* and the thistle motif in the fireplace surround of his Ramsay Garden dining room. He further sealed the alliance with France when he co-founded the Franco-Scottish Society in 1895, commissioning the painting by John Duncan, *Jehanne d'Arc et sa Garde Ecossaise* to mark the occasion.

The present volume of essays was occasioned by the exhibition *Patrick Geddes: The French Connection,* held at the Scottish National Portrait Gallery from 17 January to 18 April 2004. The premise for the exhibition was that Geddes's contacts with France and the French played an important, hitherto under-researched, role in shaping his world view. Studied mainly until now from the viewpoint of urban planning and sociology, fields in which he certainly made his mark, Geddes's ideas have a much wider appeal. In keeping with the trends of scholarship today, we feel Geddes needs to be assessed within the broader perspective of cultural history. As authors, we all come to Geddes from different standpoints ranging from the history of 19th-century French and Scottish art and design to literature, philosophy and social history.

The exhibition and its specially-commissioned video brought together works of art, documents, letters and photographs that explore the links between Geddes, the artists and intellectuals he gathered around him, and France. The essays in this volume explore these links in detail, explaining how particular conjunctions of ideas or artistic approaches came about at specific times around the personality of Geddes. Elizabeth Cumming's essay provides an introduction and an overview of Geddes's career, underscoring the French origin of many of his key formative ideas. Frances Fowle looks at the broader context for Franco-Scottish exchange in the arts towards the end of the 19th century, within which the Francophilia of the Geddes circle rightly needs to be seen. Belinda Thomson examines three specific, albeit elusive encounters between French artists and Geddes and his circle in the 1890s, one of which was intimately involved with Geddes's later close identification with Montpellier. Siân Reynolds takes up the theme of Geddes's networks, characterising the different groups of French intellectuals, academics and politicians with whom Geddes was in touch in the 1890s and the ways in which he was able to activate these links in a productive way at the Exposition Universelle of 1900. Finally Murdo Macdonald explores the French character of *The Evergreen,* Geddes's links with radical politics and ideas, and the particular international encounters he made in Paris in 1900, many of which provided the springboard for Geddes's later activism as an urbanist in India.

This project originated as an idea presented to the Society of Friends of the Institut Français d'Ecosse and we are immensely grateful for their financial and moral support. It has been heartening to have the encouragement of three successive directors at the Institut, Jean-Marc Terrasse, Ashok Adicéam and Olga Poivre d'Arvor. The project also benefited from a Larger Research

Grant from the Carnegie Trust for the Universities of Scotland. Additional funding came from the Sir Patrick Geddes Memorial Trust and the Franco-Scottish Society. Production of the video was supported by Napier University's School of Design and Media Arts. Finally, the happy coincidence of our project with the celebration of the centenary of the *Entente Cordiale* resulted in its earning the support of the Scottish Executive, for which special thanks are due to Stuart Macdonald.

Members of Geddes's family have been most helpful and we express our thanks in particular to Claire Geddes, Marion Geddes and Roger Mears. Approaching Geddes from a French perspective has offered a route into the vast sheaves of correspondence, plans, lecture notes and images that he left to posterity. His archives have been distributed, for historic reasons, between the University of Strathclyde, the University of Edinburgh and the National Library of Scotland, and the cataloguing labours of earlier Geddes scholars – in particular Dr Volker Welter and Sofia Leonard – have made the daunting task of finding one's way through this material much easier. Whilst pursuing our research, we have been treated with immense kindness and patience by many archivists and librarians in all three institutions. We wish to express our particular thanks to Olive Geddes and Dr Joseph Marshall at the National Library of Scotland; Dr Jim McGrath and Angela Seenan at the University of Strathclyde; Richard Ovenden and Arnott Wilson at the University of Edinburgh Special Collections. In addition we were helped by staff at the Royal Commission on the Ancient and Historical Monuments of Scotland, the City of Edinburgh Central Library, the library of the Museum of Scotland, SCRAN, the University of St Andrews and the Archive Service at the University of Dundee. Our thanks go to Katrina Thomson at the National Trust for Scotland and to David McAllister who, with John Colquhoun of Stuart and Stuart WS, facilitated our access to Geddes's apartment in Edinburgh. Our special thanks to Robert, Ann and Frank Naismith and to Dr Michael Shea for their forbearance in allowing a film crew to take footage of the murals at Ramsay Garden and Ramsay Lodge. For patiently answering queries and offering research leads, our thanks to Colin Harrison and his colleagues at the Ashmolean Museum, Oxford; Val Hunter, Christopher Baker, Helen Smailes and Penny Carter at the National Gallery of Scotland; Sara Stevenson and Helen Watson at the Scottish National Portrait Gallery; Dr Louise Boreham; Robin Rodger, Perth Art Gallery; Alan Johnston and Professor Ian Howard, Edinburgh College of Art; Henry Naulty, Royal Botanic Garden, Edinburgh; David and Christine Windmill, Edinburgh Zoo; Anne Dulau and Professor Pamela Robertson at the Hunterian Gallery, Glasgow; Dr Claire Willsdon and Paul Stirton, University of Glasgow; Jane Munro at the Fitzwilliam Museum, Cambridge; Patrick Bourne of Bourne Fine Art, Angela McGrath at Christie's in Edinburgh. In France Joel Matthez and Thierry Bussac at the Institut de Botanique, Montpellier oversaw the examination and photography of Leenhardt's panels and Valdo Pellegrin kindly supplied further information about Leenhardt's career; Marie-France Flahault and Jean-Marie Emberger were most helpful in providing information about and photographs of Charles Flahault; Marie-Claire Demangel opened up the Château d'Assas to our enterprising research assistants Dr John and Easta Greaves; Michel Hilaire, Michel Denizot, Viviano Rossi and John Hudson alerted Mont-péllérains to the intriguing role played by Geddes in their city; and crucial directions to the Collège des Ecossais and Indian College were provided by Kenny Munro. John Kemplay provided invaluable information on John Duncan and Frankie Jenkins generously allowed us to read her unpublished thesis on the artist; Bill Mackie in Australia shared the fruits of his research into his great uncle Charles; Per Ahlander at the School of Scottish Studies introduced us to the work of Marjory Kennedy-Fraser. Mike Small kindly granted permission to reproduce his photographs and included us on his Patrick Geddes website; Norma Henderson undertook photography at short notice. Angus Macdonald, Head of School of Arts, Culture and Environment at the University of Edinburgh, Mark Jones, Director of the V&A, Professor Iain Boyd Whyte, Professor Duncan Macmillan and Michel Duchein gave valuable support, and at the Carnegie Trust our thanks go to Sir John Arbuthnott and Helen Macdonald. Last but by no means least our thanks go to all the generous lenders, without whom the exhibition would not have been possible.

Patrick Geddes: The French Connection began as a series of stimulating committee meetings fortified by tea and Elizabeth Cumming's indispensable pancakes! With all its ups and downs, it has been a pleasure working on the project with supportive colleagues. At a crucial stage Director James Holloway and Senior Curator Julie Lawson at the Scottish National Portrait Gallery agreed to take the exhibition under their curatorial wing and we are much indebted to them; Christine Thompson and Janis Adams offered a mix of support and hard-headed realism; Nye Hughes and Robert Dalrymple created elegant display material and Jan Newton devised the exhibition's imaginative, harmonious and intelligent design; Robin MacPherson guided and shaped our ideas into an informative and accessible video; finally Perilla Kinchin at White Cockade bravely undertook the current publication. Despite warning of the dire consequences of getting involved with 'that man Geddes', our long-suffering husbands, Michael Fowle and Richard Thomson, have been unfailing in their tolerance, support and encouragement.

FRANCES FOWLE AND BELINDA THOMSON

Note on references: Full details of titles given in abbreviated form will be found in the bibliography on p.101.

Patrick Geddes: A Chronology

ELIZABETH CUMMING

1854   Born 2 October in Ballater, Aberdeenshire

1875   Begins studies under T.H. Huxley at the Royal School of Mines, London

1878   Continues his studies in France (Roscoff and Paris)

1884   Publishes *John Ruskin: Economist*

1885   Establishment of the Edinburgh Social Union

1886   Marries Anna Morton and moves into a tenement apartment in the
Lawnmarket in Edinburgh's Old Town

1887   Organises first Summer Meeting of Art and Science
Birth of daughter Norah
Publishes *Every Man his Own Art Critic: An Introduction to the Study of
Pictures* for the Manchester Art Exhibition

1888   Publishes *Every Man his Own Art Critic: An Introduction to the Study of
Pictures* for the Glasgow International Exhibition

1889   Appointed to J. Martin White Chair in Botany at University College,
Dundee
Publishes *The Evolution of Sex* (with J. Arthur Thomson)
Writes on Edward Burne-Jones for *The Scottish Art Review*

1889-90,   With Anna and Norah, spends winter months in Montpellier, working at
early 1891   Institut de Botanique alongside Charles Flahault

1891   Birth of son Alasdair

1891-6   Redevelopment and conservation of Lawnmarket and Castlehill buildings

1893   Founding of Patrick Geddes & Colleagues publishing company

1895   Birth of son Arthur
Founds Franco-Scottish Society which holds inaugural meeting in
Edinburgh 1895, Paris 1896

1895-6   Publishes *The Evergreen: A Northern Seasonal* in Edinburgh, London and
Philadelphia, and *The Interpreter*

1899, 1900   Lecture tours in America include Jane Addams' Hull House, Chicago

1900   Special Summer School at the Exposition Universelle, Paris

1904   Publishes *City Development: a Study of Parks, Gardens and Culture Institutes: A Report to the Carnegie Dunfermline Trust*

1907   Meets Philip Mairet, a future biographer, and probably also Ananda
Coomaraswamy, in Chipping Campden

1910   Civic survey of Edinburgh at the Royal Academy

1911   Cities and Town Planning Exhibition in the Civics Department of the
Outlook Tower of Crosby Hall and tours to Ireland
Publishes *Evolution* (with J. Arthur Thomson)

1912-13   *Masques of Learning* performed in Edinburgh and London
Publishes *The Masque of Ancient Learning and its Many Meanings*

1913   Cities and Town Planning Exhibition wins a gold medal at the Exposition
Internationale, Ghent
Initial design for the Scottish National Zoological Park, Edinburgh

1915   Publishes *Cities in Evolution*

1915-16   Planning exhibitions in Madras, Calcutta, Nagpur and Lucknow, India

1917   Alasdair Geddes killed on active service in France
Anna Geddes dies of enteric fever in India, unaware of his death

1919   Appointed to Chair in Sociology and Civics at Bombay University: resigns
from University College, Dundee
Commissioned by the Zionist Organisation to plan the Hebrew University
at Jerusalem

1923   Publishes *Dramatisations of History* in London, Edinburgh and India

1924   Retires to France, where he founds the Collège des Ecossais in
Montpellier

1925   Design proposals for centre of Tel-Aviv

1926   Buys Château d'Assas, six miles from Montpellier

1928   Marries Lilian Brown (who dies 1936)

1930   Founds Indian College in Montpellier

1932   Receives knighthood in London
Dies 17 April in Montpellier

I. Patrick Geddes:
Cultivating the Garden of Life

ELIZABETH CUMMING

Four years after the death of Sir Patrick Geddes (1854-1932), Philip Boardman's *Esquisse de l'oeuvre educatrice de Patrick Geddes*, the first of several studies of his mentor, was published in Montpellier. The opening chapter 'Qui est Patrick Geddes?' posited how such a question, if raised in Edinburgh, Paris, New York, London or Bombay, might elicit a wide variety of replies. In Britain, the answer might be, suggested Boardman, that Geddes was a visionary, an impractical mystic. By contrast, in India he was regarded as an achiever, an urban planner of 'plans nets et concrets'. American universities, on the other hand, considered him a sociologist, albeit one with some pretty strange ideas. But in France Geddes was regarded as a 'savant' or 'un Anglais *un peu fou*'.[1]

1. Desmond Chute, *Patrick Geddes*, 1930. Scottish National Portrait Gallery, Edinburgh.

The difficulties of trying to define, or contain, Geddes have tested writers for the last century. The urbanist Lewis Mumford, Geddes's most vocal early disciple, was the first to point out the difficulties. In 1925 he also had asked, 'Who is Patrick Geddes?' in the journal *The Survey*.[2] His question was republished as the preface to the first biography of Geddes, by Amelia Defries, who in 1927 presented Geddes as a Messianic figure, referring in her title to 'the Man and his Gospel'.[3] And if one lists the definitions of Geddes that have appeared in the titles of articles and books, he certainly seems superhuman: 'the interpreter', 'peace warrior', 'pioneer of sociology', 'social evolutionist', 'ecologist', 'biologist', 'educator', 'city planner', 'cultural catalyst', 'visual thinker', and even – surely the most ambitious of all – 'maker of the future'.

Perhaps the word 'savant', or, as Siân Reynolds suggests, the 1890s term 'intellectuel', fits him more neatly than any other.[4] On the other hand it is futile, demeaning, or perhaps just plain ignorant even to think of packaging him into any neatly labelled box. Yet two related strands of his thinking position him squarely within the reflective cultural dialogue linking Scotland and France since the Enlightenment. Like Enlightenment thinkers, Geddes was concerned with the value of the individual, and specifically with a person's place and role within an evolving, collectivist society. Related to this, he developed an ultra-contemporary, dynamic intellectual relationship between time and place which physically refabricated the heart of Scotland's capital.

These ideas were shared with a number of associates including artists and architects. Towards 1900 Geddes had collaborated with a group of young, unconventionally-minded artists to produce decorative art, mural schemes and book design, including the illustrated four-volume review *The Evergreen: A Northern Seasonal* (1895-6). This published Geddes's outline of the natural laws governing the energies and evolving transformation of culture. These were ideas in part shared directly with the artists of his own circle, particularly Charles Mackie and John Duncan, and would subsequently also find a relevance for Charles Rennie Mackintosh[5] and, primarily through internationalism and Celticity, for the Scottish Colourist J.D. Fergusson.[6] This essay introduces Geddes's thinking in the 1890s, and explores how simultaneously – a concept dear to French philosopher Henri Bergson – he sought to redefine, integrate and progress ideas of tradition and modernism.

At heart Patrick Geddes was a scientist concerned with an enquiry into the nature of variation. Throughout a long career he was absorbed with issues of modernity, building links between individuality and collectivism across subject areas from science to civic planning. Through spearheading a range of publications, conferences and programmes of urban renewal, his ideas and work – and the two were inseparable – embraced the local, the national and the international. He energised artists, urbanists and academics into engaging with standards of physical and spiritual life. While later urban work reached out as far as India and Palestine, two European cities played a vital role within his life – Edinburgh and Paris. Ultimately Geddes played a unique role in activating and connecting a dialogue of visual and intellectual ideas between Scotland and France, and, in so doing, he helped to march art and culture into the modernist age.

Observing closely the raw data of the world in order to fabricate the future shaped Geddes's daily life. The roots of his thinking were quite literally at his own feet. A childhood largely spent in rural Perthshire with an introduction to gardening and nature by his father, a retired sergeant-major in the Black Watch and member of the Free Kirk, helped to define a geographical and spiritual sense of place: he later wrote of the 'fundamental vividness of rustic life'.[7] Such awareness sharply contrasted with the tedious mechanical copying of state education.

Geddes enrolled at Edinburgh University for a course in botany and the natural sciences in 1874, but was disappointed to find little analysis of living specimens. His first experience of the city must also have been one of startling and depressing contrasts. Although he spent only a week in Edinburgh before heading south (like many other Scots before and since) for the energies of London, he must have already absorbed the differences between life in the historic but now squalid Old Town, right on the doorstep of the university, and that of the New Town where professionals and academics led comfortable lives. The city's Improvement Trust, set up by Act of Parliament in 1867, had started to demolish buildings, and open up and sanitise whole sections of the Old Town, but through this process history as well as disease was in danger of being eradicated.

In 1875, at the age of 21, he attended the London classes given by T.H. Huxley. The following year he worked as a demonstrator for Huxley, an experience that further illuminated for him the power of creative education using models to communicate and link ideas great and small. Twenty years later his analytical training as a biologist, working on cell theory, would still underpin his social thinking and invest its application with the wider, general and interdependent order of nature. Balancing such scientific theory were the publications of sociologist Herbert Spencer who linked the social and natural sciences. For Spencer (as indeed for Hippolyte Taine in France), society was an organic whole which evolved through what he called a 'law of progress'.

Thanks to Huxley, Geddes had his first taste of France in 1878. He grasped the opportunity of working with Sorbonne professor Henri de Lacaze-Duthiers at his marine station at Roscoff in Brittany. The vivid experience of contributing to research on the interdependency of life forms resulted in his paper 'Sur la fonction de la chlorophylle chez les planaires vertes' published later that year by the Académie des Sciences in Paris. And, while his work was closely scientific, the experience of combining work and social life within a small Breton community, a live Celtic society, was to influence life in Edinburgh, India and Montpellier in years to come.

He was equally inspired by the intellectual and everyday life of France, mixing ideas and making connections between science, community and life. While in London he had already come across the theories of Auguste Comte, a pioneer sociologist who emphasised the core value of academic synthesis and the prime importance of sociology within the life sciences. And, while Comte's ideas were still shaping modern life – the first sociological society had been formed in Paris in 1872 by his supporters – other Parisian writers and thinkers, some of them quite old-fashioned by French standards, were also shaping Geddes's values from the late 1870s.

In Paris Geddes heard Edmond Demolins present the social geography theories of Frédéric Le Play, thus supplying him with the three key and interdependent areas for his future socio-scientific analysis of how we might live. Le Play's 'Place, Work and Folk' itself complemented Taine's cultural synthesis of 'race, milieu, moment' that would also inspire the Scot. In 1879, while Geddes was there, a second edition of Le Play's *Les ouvriers européens* appeared in the bookshops. With its principal claim that a way of life was not necessarily linked to a family's income, its text raised possibilities within social theory that would soon burn deep into Geddes's mind and practice, from the resuscitation of Edinburgh's Old Town housing in the early 1890s to advising on civic plans for Tel-Aviv in 1925. In the commentaries to the vast pageants he directed in Edinburgh (1912), London (1913) and Indore (1917) he presented an organic view of world history. His commentary pointed out that 'the three notes of the chord of Life are organism, function, and environment – i.e., in simpler human phrase, folk, work, and place'.[8] Whilst in part inspired by Taine's panoramic *Philosophie de l'Art*, Geddes was seeking to couch the past within the present and inspire the future in Le Playist terms, to awaken the imagination through personal participation to 'fuller creative activities'.[9]

However, such synthesist concerns did not immediately find an active voice. In the late 1870s and early 1880s he wrote more than 20 closely-argued scientific papers, many published in London by the Royal Society and the Zoological Society and in Edinburgh by the Botanical Society, the Royal Physical Society and the Royal Society of Edinburgh. Many were based on his research at Roscoff and concerned molluscs, chlorophyll studies and cell work. His working methods, however, were diversifying. During palaeontological and zoological work in Mexico in 1879-80 he suffered a short period of blindness. Geddes's early biographers have found that his consequent reliance on the sense of touch resulted, through feeling the astragals of a window frame, in his squared charts used as thinking tools. From this date the visual – from chart to architecture and painting – was to be not only a means of communication but a tool within the thought process.

Geddes was gradually making his name as a scientist. He worked as a demonstrator in zoology and natural history at the University of Edinburgh's Medical School and in 1889, having been turned down for Chairs in Aberdeen, Edinburgh and St Andrews, he was appointed to a part-time Chair in Botany at University College, Dundee, which he held until 1919.[10]

However, Geddes also busied himself with broadening his publications and forging personal connections. In 1884, the year in which he was to gain support for an Environmental Society for his adopted home city of Edinburgh, he was editing *Viri Illustres*, a directory of famous Edinburgh alumni, and his essay 'John Ruskin, economist' was published. Geddes, who had already written on 'Economics and statistics from the point of view of the preliminary sciences' in the journal *Nature* in 1881, admired Ruskin.[11] A generalist, and someone of Scottish ancestry, Ruskin referred to economics as a method of measuring the success or failure of society. Essentially more important to Geddes, however, was Ruskin's contention that the health of society may be measured perhaps more accurately by the state of its culture. And, while Ruskin and Geddes differed in their opinion of Darwin (who, for Ruskin, was 'simply the nucleus of all the fools in Europe'),[12] they both considered reform necessary as a remedy only when conditions demanded it.[13] Geddes also agreed with William Morris, whom he visited in February 1885 and subsequently met in Scotland, on the value to society of good everyday design, which might make appropriate reference to the past. But, as his friend the economist James Mavor noted, Geddes the evolutionist could also almost come to blows with Morris the revolutionary.[14]

The temporary blindness in Mexico led, as his younger son Arthur was to write, to the 'development of abstract thinking',[15] but it also deepened Geddes's physical awareness and sense of self. With this came a reinforced wonder at beauty but perhaps also a fear of its temporal fragility. His experience urged him on to realise beauty's potential in his home city through education and mural decoration from the mid-1880s. Importantly it also led to an increased perception of the values of the individual within the dialogue that is society.

The Edinburgh Social Union, formed in early 1885 from the seeds of his Environment Society, had as its primary twin aims not only the beautification of public buildings of the Old Town (the organic development of which Ruskin had approved in his 1853 Edinburgh lectures) but also the encouragement of self-education. Hospitals, mission halls and orphanages were decorated by artists including Charles Mackie and Phoebe Anna Traquair,[16] while classes in singing and 'experimental science' ran alongside window gardening and gymnastics, thus providing a mix of teaching and self-directed learning and development. Geddes 'believed that the child's desire of seeing, touching, handling, smelling, tasting, and hearing are all true and healthy hungers, and these should be cultivated'.[17] Like Ralph Waldo Emerson, he encouraged self-learning: in a paper 'Every man his own philosopher' Geddes advised teachers not to endeavour to 'manufacture a ready-made synthesis but make their pupils realise that every man is his own philosopher, synthesiser, moralist, art critic, and even artist and educationalist and so on up to priest and king'.[18]

By the late 1880s Geddes the educationalist, married to Anna Morton and living in a tenement in James Court since 1886, considered the individual voice vital to the development of modern culture.[19] Although 'Every man his own philosopher' was never published, his related guides to the Manchester Exhibition (1887) and the Glasgow International Exhibition (1888), *Every Man his Own Art Critic*, were issued. The reader was asked to consider in turn 'The Art of Seeing', 'The Seeing of Art' and 'The Feeling of Art' and to 'look at pictures in the painter's way'. Art was meant to relate to the spirit of life and to man's experience. As well as emphasising painting as an experience to be shared on a personal basis by each spectator, art was to be given a role within the democratic life of the community.

Artists were asked to abandon their 'endless labour on little panels, scattered hither and thither to flap idly on rich men's walls'.[20]

The following year, 1889, the new 'Professor Geddes' addressed the second meeting of the National Association for the Advancement of Art and its Application to Industry 'On national and municipal encouragement of art upon the Continent', relating recent advances in mural work in France and advocating its further application in Britain, and, of course, Edinburgh.[21] The 'Edinburgh Congress', held in the Scottish National Portrait Gallery between 28 October and 1 November 1889, had three main sections where speakers spoke on architecture, applied art or museums and national municipal encouragement of art. The range of papers was vast, with speakers coming from art institutions, private studios or Arts and Crafts practice. They sought to build bridges between all the visual arts, with more than half the time given to combined meetings of the three defined areas. Methods for bringing art and culture to the community, to enhance life, drove much of the discussion. Geddes spoke persuasively of the need for collective cultural memory and understanding, from small 'individual efforts of voluntary associations, which in turn should rise to civic, and hence also national completeness'. Architect George S. Aitken, who would restore Old Town property for Geddes's Town and Gown Association the following decade, recalled how 'individual spirit and combined effort' had sought to educate public taste.[22]

Through the 1880s Geddes maintained a balance between the self and community, encouraging both solo activity and teamwork. By the early 1890s he had divorced himself from the Social Union when, in the aftermath of the Congress, its decorative art committee decided to travel down what he saw as a traditionalist Arts and Crafts road to create a guild of handicraft concerned with British and specifically London design practice and standards. Geddes was more than ever a conscious European who enjoyed spinning complex cultural dynamics of freedom and control. While he believed wholeheartedly in the natural development of life, he was an enabler who also wanted to steer his own ship. The indivisibility of the arts, and their organic interplay with the social and physical sciences, fill his lectures and writings through the later 1880s and the 1890s, a crucial period in his life. Having moved into the heart of the Lawnmarket, he worked towards the restoration of historic Edinburgh but equally he brought the world to Scotland in the form of Summer Meetings, international conferences held annually from 1887.[23]

For Geddes, the city was seen as the ideal site of communal activity and creativity which required its inhabitants' co-operation not only to build but to maintain it. The 1890 Housing of the Working Classes Act enabled him to access Edinburgh Corporation funds to open out and rehabilitate the slums of Castlehill and the Lawnmarket and work with a team of architects towards the restoration of closes and open courts, proposals for new building complexes and the creation of communal garden spaces.[24]

2. Summer Meeting participants, New College, Edinburgh, 1891. Geddes is seated in the middle of the second row from the front, with Charles Mackie behind him. John Duncan is seated second from the left in the front row. Anna Geddes and Anne Mackie are both standing in the fourth row (third and first woman from the left respectively). Photo © Strathclyde University Archives.

Their work, notably that of Aitken, Sydney Mitchell and Stewart Henbest Capper, lovingly recreated the heart of Scotland's capital.

The debates of international scholars and even anarchists[25] he invited to his Summer Meetings of Art and Science held from 1887 variously in New College, Teviot Place and Ramsay Garden, were intended to abandon the boundaries of traditional academic classification to engage in new intellectual possibilities (Figs 2, 4, 38). During these August meetings, exhibitions by the Old Edinburgh School of Art and recitals were laid on. The Old Edinburgh School of Art, an Arts and Crafts school founded by Geddes with Duncan in 1892, aimed to grow beauty through its art and handcrafted products but its second declared function was the 'preservation and improvement of the Old Town' based on collecting 'photo-

3. John Duncan (top), Norah and Patrick Geddes, 1893. Photo © Strathclyde University Archives.

graphs, engravings, and other records' and the 'delivery of popular lectures, addressed to the general public of Edinburgh, and intended to help
the re-awakening interest of Old Edinburgh, at once from the artistic and
historical point of view, and from the practical also'.[26]

As a scientist versed in cell structure, Geddes also turned a microscope
on his world. He created the world's first 'sociological laboratory' within
the former Short's Observatory on the Lawnmarket, purchased in 1891.
Museology was moving at this time from massed displays of objects towards the simpler, didactic 'Index Museum' indicating a growth of ideas
and discovery.[27] As the Outlook Tower, the Observatory was reworked as
both symbol and a way to measure the city.[28] It was a modern, multi-
layered museum dedicated to (in descending order from the top floor down)
the local and regional, to the national, the European and, on the ground

4. Summer Meeting participants, courtyard of Ramsay Garden, 1896. Anna and
Patrick Geddes seated together, second row, centre; Charles Mackie (with child on
his knee) to right of Geddes, Anne Mackie behind him; Paul Reclus standing third
row, fifth from right. Photo © Strathclyde University Archives.

floor, the global. Right at the top, the local and the current could be studied, quite magically, on the table of its *camera obscura*. Geddes would develop similar educational towers at Crosby Hall, London, and in Montpellier.[29] Not surprisingly, he supported the geographer Elisée Reclus's planned vast terrestrial globe (Fig.41) for the 1900 Paris Exposition Universelle, an occasion where Geddes would present an extended Summer Meeting.[30] Geddes's subsequent bid for the preservation of the Exposition's national pavilions as a giant Index Museum of the World, and his plan for a pleasure park-cum-education complex for Dunfermline led on to civic planning work around the world.

Like D'Arcy Wentworth Thompson,[31] Geddes emphasised growth and form in his lectures and writings but, unusually, he was also able to work such ideas into the field of visual culture. In 1893 he formed his publishing house of Patrick Geddes & Colleagues at the Outlook Tower: this would publish his synthesist credo in its productions, above all in *The Evergreen: A Northern Seasonal* (Fig.5).[32] By the 1890s concepts of growth and change had focused more on issues of time. His ideas connected with Parisian thought: Henri Bergson's theory of the fluid nature of time emerged in his *Matter and Memory* (1896) and was developed in sympathy with Geddes during the 1900s.[33] Emile Durkheim's *Primitive Classification* (1903) would stress the rhythmic, seasonal organisation of life and work. In *The Book of Spring* Geddes wrote of the 'seasonal rhythm of the earth' and 'times of effort and of rest, of growing and of ripening'.

Geddes was thus concerned with the shaping of the future as part of 'an unbroken intellectual tradition'.[34] His design of the *Arbor Saeculorum*, 'a great tree' which had its roots 'amid the fires of life, and is perpetually renewed from them', was published in *The Book of Spring*[35] and was used for the main window in the Outlook Tower. Similarly, the exterior and interior of Ramsay Garden, the extraordinary 1892-3 complex de-

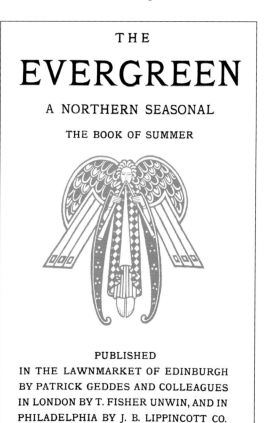

THE

EVERGREEN

A NORTHERN SEASONAL

THE BOOK OF SUMMER

PUBLISHED
IN THE LAWNMARKET OF EDINBURGH
BY PATRICK GEDDES AND COLLEAGUES
IN LONDON BY T. FISHER UNWIN, AND IN
PHILADELPHIA BY J. B. LIPPINCOTT CO.
1896

5. Title page (design John Duncan), *The Book of Summer* (1896), the third volume of *The Evergreen: a Northern Seasonal*. Photo Norma Henderson.

6. Ramsay Garden under construction, 1893-4. Riddell Collection, Scottish National Portrait Gallery.

7. Ramsay Garden seen from the west. Photo © RCAHMS.

signed by Mitchell and Capper, recorded time in space, vividly drawing the fourth dimension into its art (Figs 6, 7). Ramsay Lodge, a development by Mitchell of 18th-century pastoral poet Allan Ramsay's 'goose pie' house, conflated past and present. Capper's adjacent west block of 'speaking houses' combined a wealth of references to Scots architecture from crow-stepped gables to rounded stair towers. Exterior terracotta plaques bore mottoes that refer to the equalising power of time, from Burns's 'it's comin' yet for a' that' to (in Greek) 'as a rule, time purges everything'. Duncan's murals in the Common Room – like some painted in Geddes's own apartment at 14 Ramsay Garden – linked the past and present of national culture, with images drawn from Celtic myth, including, above the entrance, *The Awakening of Cuchullin*, symbol of the continual rebirth of culture and accompanied by the painted text 'As it hath been, so it shall be'.

In an issue of his magazine *The Interpreter*, published to decode Duncan's decoration of the Common Room of Ramsay Lodge, Geddes called it 'the vastest and most elaborate Celtic illumination in the modern world ... here are unity and contrast brought to satisfactory solution'.[36] This decoration aimed to encourage a student to explore life's possibilities, to work both singly and collectively towards the future. Introducing *The Book of Autumn* in 1895, he wrote of the need to have 'fresh readings in Life' and to look beyond the 'Autumn of our own age' to the 'approaching Spring' and of passing 'through Decadence towards Renascence'. His sweeps through history in word and image owed much to Taine, the various editions of whose *Essais de critique et d'histoire* of the late 1860s and 1870s had not only interconnected Darwinian laws governing the natural and moral sciences but, increasingly, those of the modern arts. Taine died in 1893: Geddes paid tribute in *The Evergreen*, acknowledging that his 'general idea was sound. "Life the green leaf, say we, and Art the flower". All

8. John Duncan, *Michael Scot*, 1895-6, mural panel from the Common Room, Ramsay Lodge. Scot was a 13th-century scholar and alchemist; the background is meant to represent medieval Paris. © RCAHMS.

the great flowers of literature and art rise straight from their rootstocks, each deep within its soil.'[37]

Nurturing culture for the young found support not only in Edinburgh but in Paris where in the mid-1890s, he 'was instrumental in the starting of a common residence in the Boulvard [sic] St Michel for students both French and British'.[38] From this hall his associate Marie Bonnet developed a Maison des Etudiantes into a larger residential block on the Boulevard Raspail. Geddes had wished to revive the 18th-century Franco-Scots college in Paris but in this decade he succeeded in collaboratively forming the Franco-Scottish Society.[39] Years later, on his retirement at the age of seventy from Bombay University, he did establish a Collège des Ecossais in southern France, at Montpellier.

After the heady experience of the 1900 Exposition Universelle, returning to Scotland must have seemed an anti-climax. But much work was left to be done, this time often further abroad and allowing direct engagement with world cultures. The seeds of civic thinking and cultural synthesis gathered in Paris and sown in Edinburgh were transplanted across the world, drawing Geddes equally to working with the cultures of Palestine and India where his associates respectively included the Arts and Crafts architect, designer and planner Charles Robert Ashbee[40] and the poet Rabindrinath Tagore. Encouraging a vision of world communities was deeply satisfying.[41] But the inspiration for so much of his work remained France, to which he chose to retire in 1924. There he could continue, in Voltaire's words, to cultivate his garden,[42] and observe a world in which, as he wrote, 'organic and idealist Monism is begun'.[43]

NOTES

1. Boardman, *L'oeuvre éducatrice de Patrick Geddes*, pp.11-12.

2. Lewis Mumford, 'Who is Patrick Geddes?', *The Survey*, Vol.53, 1 February 1925, New York, p.523.

3. Defries also quoted the Sermon on the Mount on the title page and John's vision from the Book of Revelation on the *verso* of the half-title. Defries, *Geddes, the Man and his Gospel*.

4. Reynolds, p.69 below.

5. See, for example, *Newsletter of the Charles Rennie Mackintosh Society*, No. 56, Summer 1991, p.8, and Macdonald, 'Patrick Geddes and Charles Rennie Mackintosh', p.12.

6. See Macdonald, p.91 below.

7. Geddes & Thomson, *Evolution*, p.112.

8. *The Masque of Ancient Learning and its Many Meanings*, Edinburgh 1913, p.31.

9. *Ibid.*, p.90.

10. Murdo Macdonald discusses the politics of the appointment within the climate of late-Victorian Dundee in his essay 'The Patron, the Professor and the Painter', *Victorian Dundee*, pp.135-50.

11. In October of that year Geddes had tried to call on Ruskin at Brantwood. NLS MS 10523 fol.208A.

12. NLS MS 10524 fol.17.

13. This ran counter to Spencer's view of the historical inevitability of reform.

14. Mavor, *Windows on the Street of the World*, Vol. 1, p.199. Mavor (p.194) commented on Morris, whom he had first met c.1884, that he 'really did not appear to regard society as a growth, but rather as a mechanical structure which might be smashed to pieces or wholly scrapped, and a new society constructed in the place formerly occupied by the old'.

15. Arthur Geddes in his entry on his father in the *Encyclopaedia Britannica*, 1949.

16. See Cumming, *Arts and Crafts in Edinburgh*, p.2. Mackie and Traquair pursued mural decoration the following decade in different directions, the former within the Geddes *coterie*, the latter relating more accurately to Arts and Crafts ideas. See Belinda Thomson, p.57 below, and E. Cumming, *Phoebe Anna Traquair 1852-1936*, Edinburgh 1993, p.23, and (with Nicola Gordon Bowe) *The Arts and Crafts Movements in Dublin and Edinburgh*, p.24.

17. Kenneth Cadenhead, 'Patrick Geddes: timeless educational ideas' in *The Educational Forum*, Vol.56, No.2, Winter 1992, West Lafayette, Indiana, p.123.

18. Unpublished paper 'Every man his own philosopher', Strathclyde University Library Geddes Archive T.GED 12/1/119/1. I am grateful to Professor Kenneth Cadenhead for drawing my attention to this Geddes lecture.

19. It is worth noting that Geddes was knighted in 1932 for his service to education.

20. *Every Man his own Art Critic*, Glasgow 1888, p.27.

21. See Fowle, p.38 below, and Thomson, p.49 below.

22. George S. Aitken, 'The architectural education of the public', *Transactions of the National Association for the Advancement of Art and its Application to Industry, Edinburgh Meeting MDCCCLXXXIX*, p.180.

23. These were subtitled Summer Schools of Art and Science.

24. All this of course cost money. Buying, restoring and letting property, even with both private and public funds, meant a shortfall in 1896 and the creation, with the help of friends, of his Town and Gown Association whose members came from across Britain. They included the Arts and Crafts bookbinder Thomas Cobden Sanderson, who had demonstrated his craft 'for working men' at in the Edinburgh congress, and his wife.

25. See Reynolds, pp.73-6 below, and Macdonald, pp.87-8 below.

26. Programme of an exhibition of the Old Edinburgh School of Art held from 9-11 April 1895. Strathclyde University Library Geddes Archive T.GED 5/1/21.

27. George Aitken referred to one proposed for the Natural History Museum, London, in 1889 and also proposed an architectural 'index' museum with 'models of buildings representing each stage of its progress from the crudest to the most complete manifestation of it, and thence onwards to its decline'. Aitken (n.22), p.181.

28. The Outlook Tower was essentially a visual encyclopaedia of life. Edinburgh, like Paris, was famous for its gathering and publication of encyclopaedia. In a sense Geddes and his associates were modern visual *encyclopédistes*.

29. Paul Reclus, nephew of Geddes's geographer associate Elisée Reclus, would establish a related Museum Centre of Human Geography in a former windmill in the village of Domme in the Dordogne in the late 1920s. My thanks to both Belinda Thomson and Michael Cuthbert for this information. See also n.30.

30. See Reynolds, p.75 below. Paul Reclus (see n.29) was given work at the Outlook Tower by Geddes in 1893. The Geddes and Reclus families were later to be formally related by the marriage of his son Arthur to a granddaughter of Elisée Reclus.

31. D'Arcy Wentworth Thompson was Professor of Zoology at University College, Dundee, then part of the University of St Andrews.

32. Geddes wrote in 'The sociology of autumn' in *The Book of Autumn* (p.28) of his aim of a 'larger view of Nature and Life, a rebuilding of analyses into Synthesis, an integration of many solitary experiences into a larger Experience, an exchange of the narrow window of the individual outlook for the open tower which overlooks college and city'.

33. In *An Introduction to Metaphysics* (English edn London 1903), Bergson, who had met Geddes by at least 1900, wrote of the mind as 'a continuous flux, a succession of states, each of which announces that which flows and contains that which precedes it'. Bergson's *L'Evolution creatrice* (Paris 1907, English edn London 1911), a philosophical study of the creative process, was published between Geddes and J. Arthur Thomson's two major publications, *The Evolution of Sex* (1889) and

Evolution (1911), and Geddes's celebrated *Cities in Evolution* (London 1911).

34. *The Evergreen: The Book of Spring*, p.14: describing Edinburgh he wrote, 'paved with history, echoing with romance, rich in an unbroken intellectual tradition – what might not this city become!'

35. *The Evergreen: The Book of Spring*, p.143.

36. *The Interpreter: Of Seven Pictures. Of Black and White*, p.14.

37. 'The sociology of autumn', *The Evergreen: The Book of Autumn*, p.31. Taine's words on life and nature were also to be paraphrased by Mackintosh (most probably in response to Geddes's essay) in his lecture 'Seemliness' (1902): '... Art is the flower – Life is the green leaf/Let every artist strive to make his flower a beautiful living thing – something that will convince the world that there may be – there are things more precious – more beautiful more lasting than life ... How Beautiful the green leaf – how beautiful life often is ...' For the full Mackintosh text see P. Robertson (ed.), *Charles Rennie Mackintosh: The Architectural Papers*, pp.224-5.

38. Unattributed typed manuscript of c.1926 in Strathclyde University Library Geddes Archive, T.GED 9/1639/2. The university quarter on the Left Bank, already popular with artists and poets, would be home to J.D. Fergusson from 1907.

39. See Reynolds, p.76 below.

40. The connections between Geddes and Ashbee are several. Like his fellow Arts and Crafts designer A.H. Mackmurdo, Ashbee had lectured to the Edinburgh Social Union, although only in 1891 after Geddes had virtually removed himself from its activities. Geddes lectured on several occasions in Chipping Campden to Ashbee's Guild of Handicraft and they subsequently worked together in Palestine. Their shared associates included Ananda Coomaraswamy, who took over Ashbee's Guild of Handicraft, and Philip Mairet, former secretary to Ashbee, who married Coomaraswamy's ex-wife Ethel. 1957 saw the London publication of Mairet's *Pioneer of Sociology: The Life and Letters of Patrick Geddes*.

41. Geddes in 1925 wrote that 'only once have I really laid hold of the imagination of a whole community – of the population of an entire city and its surrounding villages': quoted in Boardman, *The Worlds of Patrick Geddes*, p.294.

42. In fact Geddes had concluded his essay 'The sociology of autumn' in *The Evergreen: The Book of Autumn* with the words of Voltaire's Candide, 'il faut cultiver son jardin'.

43. *The Evergreen: The Book of Autumn*, p.29.

II. The Franco-Scottish Alliance: Artistic Links between Scotland and France in the late 1880s and 1890s

FRANCES FOWLE

In 1888 the Scots artist James Paterson published an article in *The Scottish Art Review* entitled 'A note on nationality in art'. In this short essay, Paterson railed against parochialism in Scottish art, exhorting artists not to 'cling to their insularity' and praising the 'sincerity and thoroughness' of French art. Above all he emphasised the importance of the French example to the development of art in Scotland.[1]

The experience of studying and working in France influenced the direction of Scottish painting in the 1880s, producing such masterpieces of realism as James Guthrie's *To Pastures New* of 1883 (Aberdeen Art Gallery) and John Lavery's modern life painting *The Tennis Party* of 1885 (Aberdeen Art Gallery). Many artists of the Glasgow School – the so-called Glasgow 'Boys' – trained in Paris or painted at Grez-sur-Loing, an artist's colony near Fontainebleau, frequented by a group of British, Irish and American artists, many of whom took their lead from Jules Bastien-Lepage (1848-1884). In the first half of the 1880s a number of Scots painters adopted the French artist's *plein-air* naturalism. Over the course of the 1890s, however, a change occurred, signalling the development in Scottish art from naturalism to decorative Symbolism. During this period there was a growing appreciation in Scotland of French art and an awareness of emerging styles such as Symbolism and Art Nouveau. Simultaneously, as part of the Arts and Crafts concept of integrating art and life and decorating buildings for the benefit of the public, there was a revival of interest in mural painting, especially the work of Pierre Puvis de Chavannes (1824-1898). As this essay will show, such developments were aided by Scots artists' continuing interest in developing trends on the Continent, as well as the intervention and encouragement of individuals such as Patrick Geddes in Edinburgh and the art dealer Alexander Reid (1854-1928) in Glasgow.

The Scottish taste for French art – specifically the work of the Barbizon School – was first manifested at the Edinburgh International Exhibition of 1886. Inspired by the Paris 'Expositions Universelles', this was the first exhibition on this scale to be held in Scotland. The Scots collector R.T. Hamilton Bruce organised a special foreign loan section, including examples of work by Corot, Daubigny and Diaz. The exhibition also included eight works by the Marseilles artist Adolphe Monticelli (1824-1886), whose arbitrary use of colour and technique of thick impasto was to have

9. George Henry, *Autumn*, 1888. © Glasgow Museums.

an important impact on Vincent van Gogh, and on the Scots artists George Henry (1858-1943) and E.A. Hornel (1864-1933).

In 1888 Glasgow was host to another International Exhibition, its first, including works by Courbet, Boudin, Degas, Bastien-Lepage and – significantly – Puvis de Chavannes. Alex Reid loaned Puvis's *Ludus Pro Patria* of 1883 (Walters Art Gallery, Baltimore), a cut-down version of the mural scheme at Amiens.[2]

Parallel to the intellectual and educational activities of Patrick Geddes in Edinburgh, Reid provided a crucial, practical link between Scots artists and French art.[3] He had a unique formation as a dealer, having lived and worked in Paris from 1886-1889 and trained alongside Theo van Gogh at the Paris firm of Boussod & Valadon. For six months he lodged at 54 Rue Lepic with Theo and his brother Vincent, whom he accompanied on occasional painting expeditions. He knew Henri de Toulouse-Lautrec and was one of the very few dealers who were always welcome in Degas's studio. He may even have met Paul Gauguin, although he did not to attempt to sell his work in Scotland until 1924.[4]

Reid returned to Glasgow in 1889 and set up his own gallery, La Société des Beaux-Arts, at 227 West George Street. From the outset he modelled himself as a French dealer, styling himself 'directeur' and retaining his Paris address, 6 Place d'Anvers, on all letterheads. Like Geddes – who, coincidentally, was born in the same year – his aim was to encourage artistic exchange between Scotland and France, exhibiting modern French art in Glasgow and later arranging exhibitions of Scottish art in Paris.[5] A contemporary and close friend of James Guthrie and Alexander Roche, Reid was also a fervent supporter of the Glasgow Boys and acted as their agent at the Munich Secession in 1890. He gave one-man shows to E.A. Hornel and Joseph Crawhall in the early 1890s and encouraged their interest in French art, specifically in Degas and Monticelli.[6]

Henry, Hornel and Monticelli

The influence of Monticelli on Hornel is generally recognised.[7] However, it is Henry who first responded to his gem-like colours and rich 'empâtement'. Roger Billcliffe has described Henry's *Autumn* of 1888 (Fig.9), as 'decorative as any mural painting' and 'the clearest indication ... of the break between Henry and Hornel and the rest of the Boys.'[8] The subject matter (a young girl in a woodland glade) and the emphasis on pattern and texture (the bold handling of paint and the way in which the figure emerges from the undergrowth, only her face distinguishable from the surrounding mosaic of colours) are closely comparable with Monticelli.

Henry may well have seen Monticelli's own painting of Autumn at the London dealer Dowdeswell & Dowdeswell, who held a retrospective exhibition of Monticelli's work in January 1888.[9] The French artist's arbitrary colour scheme, flattened perspective and discomforting lack of narrative were clearly misunderstood by a baffled and disenchanted critic of the *Art Journal*:

> Let [the onlooker] ... wander off into even the best of the ... Monticellis – for instance, the "Paysage: Automne". No sooner does he try to enter than he is brought up sharp by a distant field which rises and smacks him in the eye; the attempt to dodge round the other side of the main group of trees is similarly foiled. But, say the worshippers of Monticelli, the colour at least is lovely and unexpected. True: but you might very often say as much of a raclée ['thrashing'] de palette, and indeed some of Monticelli's pictures are no more than a suggestive old palette tickled into a faint semblance of a subject.[10]

Hornel painted his own version of *Autumn* in the same year, depicting a young girl standing in a woodland glade (Private Collection). However, despite the rough, textural handling of paint the picture lacks the 'mosaic-like', quality of Monticelli's work that Henry achieved. The merging of figure and landscape, so characteristic of the French artist, occurs only gradually in Hornel's paintings, beginning with *The Goatherd* of 1889 (Private Collection) and culminating in *The Brook* (Fig.10), in which a group

10. E.A. Hornel, *The Brook*, 1891. Hunterian Art Gallery, University of Glasgow, © The Artist's Estate.

of young girls, dressed in colourful patterned costumes, relax languidly beside a sinuous stream.

In 1890 a selection of pictures by artists of the Glasgow School was shown at the exhibition of the Munich Secession. The German art historian Richard Muther described the impact of these works in Symbolist terms:

> [T]here burst out a style of painting which took its origin altogether from decorative harmony, and the rhythm of forms and masses of colour. Some there were who rendered audacious and sonorous fantasies of colour, whilst others interpreted the poetic dreams of a wild world of legend that they had conjured

up. But it was all the expression of a powerfully excited mood of feeling through the medium of hues, a mood such as the lyric poet reveals by the eurythmical dance of words, or the musician by tones.[11]

Among the most striking images included in the exhibition were Henry's and Hornel's *The Druids* (Glasgow Art Gallery) and David Gauld's *St Agnes* (National Gallery of Scotland). Vivid colour is a distinctive feature of both paintings, as well as an emphasis on flattened forms and decorative harmony. Art historians have suggested that the artists' brilliant palette had its source in the Scottish colourist tradition, but this would hardly account for Henry's and Hornel's dramatic development in the late 1880s from dark-toned realism to the vibrant hues of their quasi-Symbolist works. Hornel, for one, admitted that he was inspired by Monticelli's use of colour.[12] From about 1888-9 onwards – in common with French artists such as Monet, Degas, Gauguin and Van Gogh – Henry and Hornel were also fascinated by Japanese colour woodblock prints, which they could see in London and Glasgow.[13]

As for Gauld's *St Agnes* and its pendant, *Music* (Hunterian Art Gallery, Glasgow), critics have suggested parallels with the work of Gauguin or Emile Bernard. It is more likely that any stylistic similarities stem from the fact that all three artists were inspired by stained-glass design. However, Gauld may have spent a brief period in France in 1889[14] and may also have heard of Gauguin's experimental style from another Scots artist, A.S. Hartrick (1864-1950), who worked in Pont-Aven from June to November 1886, lodging with Gauguin at the Pension Gloanec. (Despite their proximity, the French artist appears to have exerted little or no influence on the Scot and two key paintings by Hartrick from this period – one of Gauguin's studio and the other of a street in Pont-Aven, both in the Courtauld Institute – are distinctly naturalistic in approach.)[15] Apart from Alex Reid, who met Hartrick in Paris in 1887, there is no further evidence of any direct contacts between Scotland and Gauguin or his followers at this date. Indeed it seems that, up till 1890, although influenced by French art, Scots artists such as Henry, Hornel and even Gauld were developing their own decorative style without having set foot on French soil.

Scots artists in Brittany

After Hartrick, the first Scots artist to travel to Brittany in the late 19th century appears to have been Eric Forbes-Robertson (1865-1935), who moved to Pont-Aven in August 1890. He had attended the Académie Julian in Paris, where he lived from 1885 to 1887, returning home in the intervening period. In Pont-Aven he stayed at the Villa Julia, where he met another Scots painter, James Henry Donaldson (b.1862).[16] He also encountered Gauguin, Paul Sérusier (1863-1927), Alfred Jarry and Armand Seguin (1869-1903), who was a close friend of the Irish artist Roderic O'Conor. Two letters from Seguin to Forbes-Robertson reveal the closeness of their acquaintance, as well as the French artist's enthusiasm for Scots girls! In the second letter, written in English on 20 February 1892, Seguin confesses his desire to 'make a pilgrimage to Scotland, and get married with the "Bonniest Scotch Lassie" I can find.'[17]

Forbes-Robertson's presence at Pont-Aven was recorded by Seguin who drew him seated at a table smoking a cigarette. Gauguin may also have produced an amusing sketch (now lost) of the Scot – complete with tam o'shanter – although, given the clumsy execution, the attribution appears somewhat dubious.[18] Unlike Hartrick, who was apparently impervious to the experimental style of the Pont-Aven school, Forbes-Robertson reveals his awareness of Gauguin through the unusual viewpoint, asymmetry and crisp handling of a work such as *Great Expectations* (1894, The Central Museum and Art Gallery, Northampton), painted at Pont-Aven. He exhibited both at Pont-Aven and Rheims in 1890, 1891 and 1892 and contributed to the tenth exhibition of the Peintres Impressionistes et Symbolistes at Le Barc de Bouteville's gallery in Paris in September 1895. He also produced designs for *L'Ymagier* in 1895 and for *Le Mercure de France* in 1899.

Following in Forbes-Robertson's footsteps, the Aberdeen artist Robert Brough (1872-1905) enrolled at the Académie Julian, along with his close friend S.J. Peploe, in 1894. In Paris he could have seen work by Gauguin and his followers in various dealers' galleries, notably Le Barc de Boutteville. Gauguin was then at Pont-Aven and it seems likely that Brough visited Brittany for the first time that year.[19] Certainly, he produced his most obviously Gauguin-inspired work, *Breton Girl Herding Cattle* (Fig.11) around

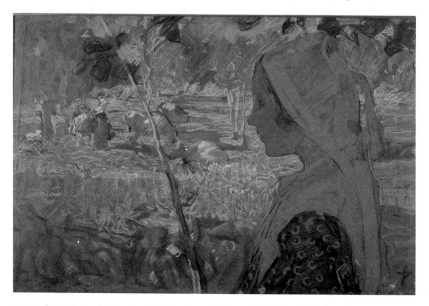

11. Robert Brough, *Breton Girl Herding Cattle*, c.1894. City of Aberdeen Art Gallery and Museums Collection.

this period. The relationship of foreground to background and the decorative treatment of the saplings in this pastel suggest an awareness of works from Gauguin's earlier Breton period, such as *Four Breton Women* of 1886 (Neue Pinakothek, Munich). The flattened, cropped forms and strong silhouette of the girl's face may also derive from Gauguin, as well as revealing the influence of Japanese art. In particular, the way in which the girl's switch divides the canvas – a device inspired by Japanese Ukiyoe prints – recalls the composition of Gauguin's *Vision of the Sermon, Jacob Wrestling with the Angel* (National Gallery of Scotland) painted in Brittany in 1888. Tantalisingly the date of Brough's work is illegible, but we know that he returned to Brittany in subsequent years, visiting Concarneau in 1896 and 1897, when he produced numerous works in oil and pastel. In Concarneau he almost certainly encountered the Lyonnais artist Achille Granchi-Taylor (1857-1921) who was resident there from 1889 onwards.[20]

Other Scots made the pilgrimage to Brittany in the 1890s. These included the female artist Stansmore Dean (1866-1944) (soon to become the second wife of Robert Macaulay Stevenson) who travelled to Brittany in the late 1890s and regularly passed the summer in the south of France. Dean's *Breton Girl* of c.1898 (Private Collection), is characterised by a limited palette, simplified forms and a certain naivety of vision, but its mood of quiet reverie and self-absorption owes more to Whistler than to Gauguin.

As the years progressed, Brough's interest in surface pattern gave way to a more fluid, realist style of painting which drew on a variety of sources including Velasquez, Sargent and Whistler. Nevertheless, known for his avant-garde tendencies, he was invited to contribute to the Summer 1896 edition of Geddes's *Evergreen*. He produced a wood engraving entitled *Roses* (Fig.12). Disappointingly, despite its 'Breton' subject – a Breton woman and her child seated in an imaginary landscape – it lacks the audacity of the earlier *Breton Girl Herding Cattle*. Certainly it reveals a concern for rhythmic lines and surface pattern, but without the simple, primitive forms of, say, Mackie's or Sérusier's work.

12. Robert Brough, *Roses*, from *The Evergreen, The Book of Summer*, 1896, p.9. © National Library of Scotland.

French sources for John Duncan and *The Evergreen*

The Evergreen provided a unique vehicle for the dissemination of Patrick Geddes's theories, especially the notion of 'synthesis' – not only of arts and crafts, but of science and socialism, ideas which were nurtured and reinforced by his artistic and anarchist contacts in France.[21] The pages of *The Evergreen* are testament to the close cultural and intellectual links that Geddes forged between the two countries in the mid-1890s. Not only did the journal publish articles by French savants such Elisée Reclus, Charles Sarolea and the Abbé Félix Klein, and illustrations by Paul Sérusier, it included prints and drawings by Scots artists inspired by French art. The Summer 1896 edition, for example, included a line drawing by John Duncan (1866-1945) entitled *The Way to Rheims* (Fig.47), a design for his *Jehanne d'Arc et sa Garde Ecossaise* (Fig.13), commissioned by the Franco-Scottish Society in 1895.[22] The subject may have been indirectly inspired by the competition for the stained glass windows of Orléans Cathedral in 1893, when the chosen subject was the major episodes in the life of Joan of Arc. Duncan may even have seen the controversial designs of the French artist Eugène Grasset (1845-1917), which, although rejected, were widely publicised.[23]

13. John Duncan, *Jehanne d'Arc et sa Garde Ecossaise*, c.1895. City Art Centre, Edinburgh.

Along with Charles Mackie (discussed by Belinda Thomson, pp. 52-64), John Duncan was one of Patrick Geddes's closest collaborators. In 1892 he assisted Geddes in the establishment of the University Hall School of Art, subsequently known as the Old Edinburgh School of Art, of which he was first Director.[24] Guided by Geddes's principal of 'synthesis', the curriculum offered examination-free, practice-based teaching on a wide range of courses, from embroidery, bookbinding and Celtic design to history and literature. Inspired by Geddes's ideas, Duncan aimed to breathe new life into Scottish painting, through a bringing together of different artistic styles and cultures. He personally favoured a fusion of Celtic (and often Classical) mythology and French Symbolist theories. It could therefore be said that a new 'nationalist' art resulted from the marriage of French 'synthetist' theories – the primacy of colour, line and form over subject – and Geddesian 'synthesis'.

Working closely with Geddes on several projects, including *The Evergreen*, Duncan provided some of the journal's most innovative designs. These include *Bacchus and Silenus* (Fig.14), a reproduction of one of eight panels commissioned by Geddes for his flat in Ramsay Garden.[25] Much of the decorative scheme, illustrating 'The Evolution of Pipe Music', was painted over in the 1930s, but Duncan's murals were described and partly reproduced in contemporary journals, revealing a fusion of Classical and

14. John Duncan, *Bacchus and Silenus*, from *The Evergreen, The Book of Autumn*, 1895, pp.90-1. © National Library of Scotland.

Celtic legends, incorporated in a dynamic Art Nouveau design.[26] Almost all the panels were in place by 1895, including the Bacchanalian procession. Duncan conceived the idea for this panel as early as March 1893[27] and it was probably while working on the project that he first became aware of the work of Eugène Grasset. In particular, a Grasset watercolour entitled *La Muse Druidique*, reproduced in *L'Art et L'Idée* in October 1892,[28] depicts a scantily dressed maiden with flowing hair and robes, closely resembling the female maenad in Bacchus's embrace on the right of Duncan's image.

In 1894 Grasset held an important one-man exhibition in Paris, organised by La Plume, in which his frieze design, *Harmonie* (Musée d'Orsay, Paris) was shown. Assuming he saw the exhibition, Duncan may have taken the idea of combining wild animals with figures playing musical instruments from the cortège in Grasset's design. On the other hand, Duncan's musicians express an abandon and exuberance that is quite lacking in Grasset's more sedate, Botticelli-inspired procession. Indeed one of the female figures in Duncan's panel may even have inspired Sérusier, who included a similar figure clad in a leopard skin in *Danse Champêtre*, the mural scheme which he designed for his own dining-room.[29]

Another contributor to *The Evergreen*, and an important exponent of Geddes's ideas was Robert Burns (1869-1941), who would also be closely associated with the Edinburgh College of Art. A number of his illustrations pay homage to the English Aestheticism pervading the pages of *The Yellow Book*. (*Vintage*, for example, reproduced in *The Evergreen* '*Book of Autumn*' in 1895, p.23, combines an aesthetic, Leightonesque subject with the patterns and arabesques of Aubrey Beardsley.) However, like Duncan, his most innovative illustration for *The Evergreen*, *Natura Naturans* – originally designed in 1891 – represents a unique fusion, not only of Classical and Celtic mythology, but of the decorative forms of Celtic art, Japanese prints and Art Nouveau.[30]

Clare Willsdon has suggested that, like Duncan's *Bacchus and Silenus*, many of the illustrations reproduced in *The Evergreen* were records of Geddes's mural scheme for his flat in Ramsay Garden.[31] She includes among these Burns's *Vintage*, *Passer-by* and *Bathers*, Mackie's *Lyart Leaves* (Fig.31) and *Felling Trees*, Brough's *Roses* and Hornel's *Madame Chrysanthème* (Fig.46). The last was reproduced in the *Book of Autumn* in 1895. It was probably through Mackie or Pittendrigh Macgillivray that Hornel was invited to contribute to *The Evergreen*,[32] but his work may have been brought to Geddes's attention through his first one-man exhibition of Japanese pictures, held at Alex Reid's gallery in the spring of 1895. Known for his close associations with Japanese culture (he and Henry had spent 18 months in Japan between 1893 and 1894), Hornel chose to contribute a drawing of a geisha looking across an ornamental garden. Although Japanese in subject the choice of title was French in origin, since it makes direct reference to Pierre Loti's novel of the same name. Pierre Loti was the pen name of Julien Viaud, whose novels were an inspiration for both Vincent van Gogh and Paul Gauguin. Van Gogh was reading *Madame Chrysanthème* when he moved to Arles in February 1888 and it may have been Viaud's *Le Mariage de Loti* which suggested to Gauguin the idea of travelling to Tahiti in 1891.

Puvis de Chavannes and the revival of mural painting in Scotland

Although figures such as Gauguin, Sérusier and Grasset were an important source for the Scots artists who contributed to *The Evergreen*, the French artist Puvis de Chavannes was of even greater significance to the development of mural painting in Scotland throughout this period. The repeated rhythms, two-dimensional composition and (despite the strong colourist tradition in Scottish painting) the pale tonality of his work were greatly admired by a number of Scots artists. In 1890 John Duncan visited Paris and saw the Sainte Geneviève murals at first hand. His reaction was mixed. He admired Puvis's pale colours, subtle modulations of tone and atmospheric effects, but was disappointed by the resolution of forms, dismissing one figure in particular as 'a little wishy-washy'.[33] The Glasgow artist Alexander Roche (1861-1921), on the other hand, admired Puvis's muted palette and was influenced by his work as early as 1887.

15. Pierre Puvis de Chavannes, *Vigilance*, 1867. National Gallery of Scotland, Edinburgh.

Roche first encountered Puvis in 1882, while studying at the Académie Julian in Paris along with John Lavery (1856-1941). Roche later recalled that during that period '... ardour and tobacco burned freely before the shrines of Puvis de Chavannes and Jules Bastien-Lepage.'[34] While Lavery was more instantly drawn to Bastien-Lepage, Puvis's influence is evident in Roche's masterpiece, *Good King Wenceslas* of 1887 (Private Collection), exhibited at the Munich Secession in 1890. The colours are muted and pale, the sparse landscape and stylised trees recall the setting of Puvis's *L'Enfance de Sainte Geneviève* (1877) and *Jeune Picards s'exerçant à la lance* (*Ludus Pro Patria*), which he could have seen at the 1882 Salon.

Roche was a close friend of Alex Reid (he even introduced Reid to his first wife) and may have communicated his interest to the dealer. During his stay in Paris Reid bought at least two pictures by Puvis: a pastel portrait of a woman[35] and the cut-down version of *Ludus Pro Patria*. The latter had remained unsold from an exhibition of 82 works by Puvis held at Durand-Ruel's in November 1887. Enthused by the exhibition, Reid scribbled down notes for a review which was never published. The review was written half in French and half in English and later translated by Reid's son, A.J. McNeill Reid.[36] It reveals a deep and genuine love of the artist, which was apparently quite unaffected by commercial considerations.[37]

Reid was swift to encourage the Scots' enthusiasm for Puvis. His first major exhibition of French art, which opened in London in December 1891 and in Glasgow in February 1892, included several works by France's foremost mural painter, as well as Monet, Degas, Pissarro and Whistler. We have no record of which pictures by Puvis might have been included, but we do know that one of Reid's clients, Arthur Kay, owned a study for Puvis's *Vigilance* (Fig.15),[38] which formed part of a decorative scheme of 1866 for the Hôtel Vignon in Paris. The female allegorical figure in this painting holds a torch aloft in her right hand, a symbol of artistic inspiration and illumination. In 1894 Puvis used the figure of the torchbearer again at the Hôtel de Ville in Paris to symbolise cultural enlightenment, a suitably Geddesian image.

Indeed, it was largely as a result of Patrick Geddes's intervention that an interest in Puvis was fostered in both Glasgow and Edinburgh during the 1890s, especially by those involved in public decorative schemes. In 1889 Geddes delivered a paper entitled 'On national and municipal encouragement of art upon the Continent' to the Edinburgh Art Congress.[39] In October of the same year, a Paris-based acquaintance of Geddes, Cecil Nicholson published an article in the *Scottish Art Review* on the 'Municipal encouragement of art in Paris',[40] commenting on the important role of the city in funding public decorative schemes. In particular the article focused on 'the exterior and interior decoration of the new Hôtel de Ville, the new Mairies' and 'the new Sorbonne ... half ... at the expense of the State, ... half at the expense of the city of Paris,'[41] and stressed the importance of preserving such important symbols of civic life.

A growing sense of civic responsibility, together with an increasing awareness of the importance of Puvis de Chavannes encouraged the City of Glasgow to send a deputation of officials to Paris to inspect the new decorative scheme at the Sorbonne, the Panthéon and the Hôtel de Ville, as well Puvis de Chavannes' murals in Amiens.[42] Their enthusiastic report was presented in 1894 and Roche, Henry, E.A. Walton (1860-1922) and Lavery were commissioned to design murals illustrating Glasgow's past for the Banqueting Hall of the new City Chambers. These were complemented by William Findlay's Scottish rivers personified as floating women, which show a clear debt to Puvis. Similarly E.A. Walton's preparatory sketch for the unexecuted mural, *The Burial of Fergus* (Fig.16) – a subject also tackled by John Duncan in his mural scheme for Geddes's Ramsay Lodge – reveals an

16. E.A. Walton, *The Burial of Fergus*, 1902, sketch for an unexecuted mural for the City Chambers, Glasgow. Hunterian Art Gallery, University of Glasgow.

awareness of the Sorbonne murals and the St Genevieve cycle in the Panthéon. By contrast Lavery's *Modern Shipbuilding*, with its contemporary subject matter, was probably inspired by the iconography of the Paris Mairies, as well as drawing on William Bell Scott and modern Japanese sources.[43]

Interest in Puvis was increased in 1896 by the publication by Patrick Geddes & Colleagues of four lithographic reproductions of the Sainte Geneviève panels.[44] This was possibly in response to Gabriel Mourey's article on Puvis published in *The Studio* in March 1895. In consecutive years a plethora of articles and essays followed, appearing in the *Art Journal* (1896), *Art Amateur* (1897) and the *Athenaeum* (1898). Such was the primacy of Puvis, contemporary commentators were apt to ascribe his influence even when it was not wholly evident. William Hole's decorative scheme for the Scottish National Portrait Gallery, for example, was frequently compared to Puvis by contemporary commentators.[45] Certainly the *St Columba* panel is close to the French artist in its muted tones and flattening of space. And as Helen Smailes has pointed out, the spirit fresco medium that Hole adopted for much of the decorative scheme (namely the processional frieze and the historical murals) was similar to Puvis's 'wax painting' technique.[46] But here the resemblance ends, and the murals lack the allegorical subject matter, repeated rhythms and withdrawn, disengaged figures of Puvis's best-known works. On the other hand, the composition of the *Battle of Bannockburn* may well have been inspired by another French source: Louis-Maurice Boutet de Monvel's *La Vie de Jeanne d'Arc*, published in Paris in 1896, of which Geddes owned a copy.

17. (Left) John Duncan, *Anima Celtica*, c.1895. National Trust for Scotland.

18. John Duncan, *Anima Celtica*, from *The Evergreen, The Book of Spring*, 1895, p.107. © National Library of Scotland.

John Duncan's mural paintings and French Symbolism

John Duncan's most Puvis-inspired work is without doubt *Anima Celtica* (Fig.17) which relates closely to the line drawing reproduced in the Spring 1895 edition of *The Evergreen* (Fig.18). Both pictures include a central female figure, tentatively identified by Murdo Macdonald as the Celtic goddess Bride.[47] In the painted version Celtic mythology has been elided with Puvis's Symbolism to produce a multi-layered image. Puvis's influence is most evident in the muted colour and flat treatment of space and, more specifically, in the female figure in the top left-hand corner. The identity of this figure is unclear. The presence of the three doves recalls Geddes's own insignia, but the addition of the eagle evokes Puvis's allegorical figure of 'La France', depicted in *The Carrier Pigeon* (1871, Musée d'Orsay, Paris). She is possibly also an unconventional representation of Beira, the Celtic Goddess of Winter (more usually represented as an old hag) who regained her youthful appearance at the Spring equinox. The figure at top right is Mannan, God of the Irish Sea, whose swine (hence the dying boar on the left of the composition) constantly renewed themselves. Renewal and rebirth is therefore an important theme of this picture, aptly illustrating Geddes's and Duncan's commitment to the Celtic Renaissance.

In 1898 Duncan showed his painting *Mythological Subject (The Sorceress)* (Fig.19) at the Dundee Fine Art Exhibition. The generic nature of the title perhaps hinted that its sources were wider than merely Celtic mythology, drawing attention to the parallels that exist across different cultures. The exotic setting, brilliant colours and decorative treatment are comparable with Gauguin's own depictions of Polynesian mythology, while the dark-haired weeping women have affinities with those in Sérusier's *Melancholy* of c.1890. Duncan may well have seen Durand-Ruel's exhibition of Gauguin's Tahitian pictures in Paris in November 1893, and examples of both Gauguin and Sérusier were shown in mixed Nabi shows at Le Barc de Boutteville.

19. John Duncan, *Untitled Mythological Subject*, 1898. University of Dundee Museum Services.

Above all else, it is Duncan's decorative scheme for Henry Beveridge at Pitreavie Castle in Dumfermline that reveals the extent of his knowledge of French avant-garde art. A Bacchanalian procession, with flattened, decorative forms, reappears in Duncan's watercolour designs for the murals, which depict the legend of Orpheus. Duncan may have looked to Grasset's *La Muse Druidique*, mentioned above, as a source for the main figure. Grasset's watercolour features a half-naked, lyre-playing muse, close to Duncan's own lithe Orpheus.

The watercolour designs (Fig.20) were reproduced in an article by Margaret Armour, published in *The Studio* in 1897.[48] Armour compared Duncan's designs to those of Puvis, drawing attention to the light tonality of his work and the way in which he respected the flat plane of the wall. She also commented, however, that, in contrast to Puvis, Duncan's 'arrangements are more ornamental ..., and his ornament is more employed in detail ... Classic restraint marks his composition and technique, while

20. John Duncan, *Orpheus and Eurydice*, 1895, preparatory study for mural decoration at Pitreavie Castle, Dunfermline. Private Collection.

the dramatic intensity of his treatment betrays the fervour of the Celtic temperament.'[49]

Clearly Duncan, in his search for a style of painting that would adequately express the eclecticism and modernity of Scottish art, was drawing on a wider range of sources than Puvis. Like the Glasgow artists he was aware of Celtic art, Japonisme and developments in stained glass design, but he was also almost uniquely in tune with the work of the French Symbolists and, during the 1890s, immersed himself in the theories of Sâr Péladan and the Salon de la Rose + Croix.[50]

The tragic story of Orpheus and Eurydice appealed to the Symbolist temperament, especially the part of the legend illustrated in the third panel of Duncan's mural scheme. Having lost Eurydice by turning back and catching a glimpse of her as they escaped from the Underworld, Orpheus was torn to pieces by Thracian women celebrating the Bacchic revels, and his head was thrown into the river Hebrus. The head of Orpheus continued to lament the loss of Eurydice as it floated down to the Aegean Sea. Artists regarded the severed but still singing head as an image of the immortality of art. The theme not only inspired Symbolist artists such as Puvis and Gustave Moreau but the Belgian artist Jean Delville (1867-1953),[51] whose *Head of Orpheus* (1893, Private Collection) is a likely source for the image at the bottom of Duncan's watercolour. Delville lived in Paris and exhibited this work and *Angel of Splendour* (1894, Private Collection, Brussels) at Sâr Péladan's Salons de la Rose + Croix in 1893 and 1894. The rhythmic lines of Duncan's composition and the writhing, helpless body of Orpheus in the middle panel of the watercolour design bear more than a passing resemblance to the forms in Delville's *Angel*, especially the figure caught up in the transparent waves of the angel's dress.[52]

The Salons de la Rose + Croix were an important source for Duncan, whose eclectic style reveals the influence not only of Delville, but of other Rosicrucians such as the Belgian artist Fernand Khnopff (1858-1921), whose work was frequently reproduced in *The Studio* in the early 1890s. Duncan's *Head of a Celtic God* (Private Collection) and *Female Head* (Dundee Art Galleries and Museums) clearly derive from Khnopff's *Closed Eyes*, the title referring to the subconscious or 'inner vision', a favourite theme of Symbolist artists.

The fusion of avant-garde art and Celtic imagery is not unique to Duncan: other Scots artists such as Charles Rennie Mackintosh and the Macdonald sisters drew on Rosicrucian sources, including Carlos Schwabe, with whom they were acquainted, and Jan Toorop, whose esoteric *The Three Brides* was reproduced in *The Studio* in 1893.

The cross-fertilisation of ideas that took place in Scotland during the 1890s resulted in the fruition of a truly international style of painting. In 1900 John Duncan lectured alongside Patrick Geddes at the Exposition Universelle in Paris; in the same year Charles Rennie Mackintosh and his contemporaries were prominent at the 8th Vienna Secession; and the following year French artists were represented by over 140 paintings at the International Exhibition in Glasgow.

By 1901 James Paterson no longer had cause to rail against the parochialism of Scottish art. While Alex Reid in Glasgow provided a practical link with Europe through the importation and exhibition of French pictures, Geddes in Edinburgh raised intellectual awareness through his writing, personal networking and through communal projects such as *The Evergreen* and the decorative schemes for Ramsay Lodge. As a result individual artists like John Duncan were persuaded to travel abroad and observe French art at first hand.

Geddes, like Paterson, celebrated the internationalist approach of Scots artists in the late 19th century and regarded the infiltration of French (and especially Breton) art and literature into Scottish culture as a vital feature of the Celtic Renaissance. In the early years of the 20th century J.D. Fergusson (1874-1961) followed in Geddes's footsteps, achieving a similar fusion of Celtic and French (specifically Fauve) art. Fergusson's art has been described in terms of 'a longing for, rather than an imminent arrival at, a native identity in Scottish painting'. Similarly, Peploe, by embracing French art, has been accused of 'turning his back on the native elements of his culture.'[53] Yet both artists, like Geddes and Paterson, and like the artists in Geddes's circle, eschewed parochialism in favour of a broader, Celtic identity, which they achieved through a synthesis of French and Scottish art.

NOTES

1. James Paterson, 'A note on nationality in art', *Scottish Art Review*, Vol.1, 1888-9, pp.89-90.

2. Exhibited as *Ancient Picards Practising with Lances* (no.1654). Reid bought this work from Durand-Ruel on 1 March 1888 for 5,000 francs.

3. See Frances Fowle, *Alexander Reid in Context: Collecting and Dealing in Scotland in the Late 19th and Early 20th Centuries*, unpublished PhD thesis, University of Edinburgh 1993.

4. According to Margaret Peploe, Reid did know Gauguin. See Hardie, *Scottish Painting*, pp.98-9.

5. Reid organised an exhibition of the Scottish Colourists at the Galerie Barbazanges in Paris in 1924.

6. Reid was referred to affectionately by the some of the 'Boys' as both 'Degas Reid' and 'Monticelli Reid'. Henry refers to the dealer as 'Monticelli Reid' in a letter to Hornel, dated 17 March 1892, ref 2/18, E.A. Hornel Library, Broughton House, Kirkcudbright.

7. R. Billcliffe, *The Glasgow Boys. The Glasgow School of Painting 1875-1895*, London 1985, pp.207-8; W. Hardie, 'E.A. Hornel reconsidered', *Scottish Art Review*, Vol.11, No.3, 1968, pp.19-21, 27-8; Bill Smith, *Hornel. The Life and Work of Edward Atkinson Hornel*, Edinburgh 1997, pp.42-4.

8. Billcliffe, (n.7), p.239.

9. There are several references in the Henry–Hornel correspondence to projected visits to London, but the letters are undated and few details are mentioned.

10. 'Exhibitions: Monticelli', *Art Journal*, 1888, p.94.

11. Richard Muther, *A History of Modern Painting*, English trans. 1896, quoted in Billcliffe (n.7), p.297.

12. Edward Pinnington wrote in 1900 that Hornel acknowledged the influence on his work of Monticelli, 'whom he studied for colour, and whom at his best he considers a great painter'. See Edward Pinnington, 'Mr E.A. Hornel', *Scots Pictorial*, 15 June 1900, p.173.

13. Fowle (n.3), pp.88-9

14. Anna Gruetzner in *Post-Impressionism*, Royal Academy, London, 1979-80, p.189, asserts that Gauld studied in Paris that year.

15. Hartrick spent the following year in Paris, where he met Van Gogh and Alex Reid, before returning to Scotland at the end of 1887. See Martin Bailey, 'Memories of Van Gogh and Gauguin: Hartrick's Reminiscences', *Van Gogh Museum Journal*, 2001, pp.97-105.

16. Donaldson was in Pont-Aven from 1885 to 1895 and exhibited there in 1894.

The exhibition catalogue included a preface and illustrations by Seguin. Information kindly provided by Belinda Thomson.

17. The letter is reproduced in Denys Sutton, 'Echoes from Pont-Aven', *Apollo*, Vol.79, No.27, May 1964, p.406.

18. The Seguin drawing is included in a sketchbook which is in the Forbes-Robertson family. See Sutton (n.17), pp.403-6; reproduced on p.404. The Gauguin drawing is reproduced on p.405.

19. Jennifer Melville, *Robert Brough 1872-1905*, Aberdeen 1995, p.16.

20. Two pastels by Brough, *The Harbour, Concarneau* (Private Collection), and *Breton Girl* (Private Collection) are dated 1896 and 1897 respectively.

21. On Geddes's notion of 'synthesis' see Elizabeth Cumming, 'A "Gleam of Renaissance Hope": Edinburgh at the turn of the century', in Wendy Kaplan (ed.), *Scotland Creates: 5000 Years of Art and Design*, Glasgow 1990, pp.152-3. For Geddes's anarchist contacts in France see Reynolds below, pp.73-6.

22. See letter from Geddes to Duncan, November 1895 in which he notes a suggestion from Andrew Lang for a painting of Joan of Arc with her bodyguard of Scottish Archers, quoted in Macdonald below p.93, n.11.

23. See *De l'Impressionisme à l'art nouveau: Acquisitions du musée d'Orsay 1990-1996*, Paris 1996, p.210. I am grateful to Belinda Thomson for pointing out the Grasset connection.

24. I am grateful to Frankie Jenkins for allowing me access to her unfinished PhD thesis, *The Life and Career of John Duncan*, University of Edinburgh. For further information on Duncan, see John Kemplay, *The Paintings of John Duncan, A Scottish Symbolist*, San Francisco 1994.

25. Reproduced in the *Book of Autumn*, 1895, pp.90-1.

26. Margaret Armour, 'Mural decoration in Scotland, Part I', *Studio*, Vol.10, 1897, pp.101-4 and 'The decorative paintings of John Duncan', *Artist*, Vol.21, 1898, pp.146-52.

27. It is described in a letter to Sir William Craigie, 25 March 1893, National Library of Scotland, Acc.9987/32.

28. Octave Uzanne, 'Eugène Grasset', *L'Art et L'Idée*, No.10, 20 October 1892, pp.192-220, repr. p.201.

29. This figure's clothing differs in the *Evergreen* reproduction, where she is dressed in a material decorated with crosses, rather than spots. Clare Willsdon suggests, that Sérusier may have had first-hand knowledge of Geddes's flat. See Willsdon, 'Paul Sérusier the Celt', *Burlington Magazine*, Feb. 1984, pp.88-91.

30. Published in the *Book of Spring* in 1895, p.27.

31. Willsdon, *Mural Painting*, p.322, n.71.

32. Smith, *Hornel* (n.7), p.98.

33. John Duncan Archive, National Library of Scotland, Notebook 1, p.9.

34. Shaw Sparrow, *John Lavery and his Work*, London [1911], pp.40-1, quoted in K. McConkey, *Sir John Lavery*, Edinburgh 1993, p.21.

35. Sold to Paul Durand-Ruel in December 1888 for 300 francs.

36. McNeill Reid file, National Library of Scotland.

37. 'There closes here tomorrow an Exhibition, the memory of which will long dwell in the hearts of those who have been fortunate enough to be allowed to regard and appreciate it, the Exhibition of the works of Puvis de Chavannes in the Galeries Durand-Ruel, Rue Peletier.
The gathering together of those works could have but one effect, to increase the

number of those who justly esteem him as the foremost French artist. The sensation on entering this exhibition is as if, from the heart of Paris in the 19th century, one had been instantaneously transported back to Ancient Greece ... In the course of conversation one day with one of the chiefs of the new school, a sworn enemy to the allegories of former times, the name of Puvis de Chavannes happened to be mentioned, and he could not help speaking of him with emotion. I was curious to hear how he could reconcile his praise of Puvis with his own artistic convictions. "True," said he, "I admit I am inconsistent mais que voulez-vous? His theories are the contrary of mine, yet his art seduces me; his aesthetic principles I detest and his works enchant me all the same. I don't understand it but I am carried away in spite of myself." And he was right.' It is tempting to speculate that Reid's artist friend was Degas, whom the dealer greatly admired.

38. This picture was included in a sale at Sotheby's, London on 29 October 1970 (cat.8).

39. Sir Patrick Geddes Archive, Strathclyde University Archives, Glasgow, 1889, p.8.

40. C. Nicholson, 'Municipal encouragement of art in Paris', *Scottish Art Review*, Vol.2, June – Dec. 1889, London 1889, pp.209-10.

41. Nicholson (n.40), p.209.

42. Willsdon, *Mural Painting*, p.184

43. Willsdon, *Mural Painting*, p.184. See also W. Buchanan, 'The Asahi restored' in *Journal of the Scottish Society for Art History*, Vol.6, 2001, pp.77-80.

44. In 1896 these four lithographic reproductions were published in Paris, scaled down from a poster by Alexandre Lauzet. See Thomson below, p.66, n.5.

45. See article in *The Scotsman*, 6 November 1901.

46. Helen Smailes, *A Portrait Gallery for Scotland, The Foundation, Architecture and Mural Decoration of the Scottish National Portrait Gallery 1882-1906*, Edinburgh 1985, p.54.

47. M. Macdonald, 'Anima Celtica: embodying the soul of the nation in 1890s Edinburgh', in T. Cusack and S. Bhreathnach-Lynch (eds), *Art, Nation and Gender: Ethnic Landscapes, Myths and Mother-Figures*, Ashgate 2003, pp.1-10.

48. Included in Christie's Scottish Sale, 28 October 1999 (lot 236).

49. Armour (n.26), pp.101-4.

50. To which he makes reference in his Notebooks, National Library of Scotland. See Willsdon, *Mural Painting*, p.327.

51. For biographical information on Delville, see Olivier Delville, *Jean Delville, peintre 1867-1953*, Éditions Laconti, 1984.

52. Delville has intriguingly close links with Scotland, since he taught at Glasgow School of Art from 1900 to 1906 and was even made director for a brief period. He exhibited work at the Royal Glasgow Institute in 1902 when he showed *Orphans* (cat.7) and in 1904, when he showed *The Love of Souls* (1900, Musée d'Ixelles, Brussels) (ex. cat.) and a portrait of Mrs J.W.M. Webb (cat.39). During this period he lived at 42 Kersland Street, Glasgow. He was later made director of the Académie Royale des Beaux-Arts in Brussels, where he remained until 1937.

53. Tom Normand, 'Scottish modernism and Scottish identity' in Wendy Kaplan (ed.), *Scotland Creates: 5000 Years of Art and Design*, Glasgow 1990, pp.164-5.

III. Patrick Geddes's 'Clan d'Artistes': Some Elusive French Connections

BELINDA THOMSON

> Il y a autour de Geddes tout un clan d'artistes ... Ce qu'il faut ... c'est entretenir des relations d'amitié avec tous ces jeunes, comme nous, pleins d'ardeur et d'enthousiasme.*
>
> Auguste Hamon to Lucien Pissarro, Edinburgh, February 1895

One might suppose Patrick Geddes, trained as a biologist and practically engaged in the teaching of botany, to have had no more than a passing and amateurish interest in the visual arts. On the contrary, as a generalist thinker by vocation, a practitioner of the synthesis of ideas, Geddes was a passionate advocate of art's intrinsic relationship to life. At the outset of his career he made it his business to take an active and practical role in studying and commenting upon contemporary painting, promoting art's vital role in education and providing conditions conducive to its practice. Within the arts he worked not only as a critic and theorist but as catalyst and patron. As other essays show, his artistic ambitions for Edinburgh took concrete form in activities as diverse as publishing, in commissioning (or encouraging others to commission) mural schemes for public and private buildings, and in organising summer schools involving series of lectures and dramatic masques. Although in developing his aesthetic ideas Geddes was strongly influenced by contemporary currents in Britain, notably by John Ruskin, William Morris and the Arts and Crafts movement, he was also deeply committed to a more European outlook, and in particular to the example of France.

In 1889, Geddes took up his part-time post of Professor of Botany at the University of Dundee. That year he also addressed the Edinburgh audience of a conference on the 'Advancement of Art and its Application to Industry', the second annual congress of the Arts and Crafts movement, and used France as his chief model.[1] In France, he argued, 'art appears as the natural accompaniment of all forms of industry; not as a luxury or an afterthought as with us, but as co-extensive with life, just as hygiene should be.' Geddes's scientific training often shows through in his choice of metaphors. Who else would have likened art to hygiene, or the 'stirrings of the Civic Renaissance' for which he was ardently working to 'microscopic leaven'? Often described as an effervescent personality, Geddes's very modus operandi was consciously and consistently modelled on the process of fermentation, working from the bottom up, from individual effort towards group, communal or institutional action. His laboratory observations of the remarkable capacity of microscopic spores to multiply informed his determination to bring about a similar effect in the realm of art, architecture and the environment. All that was needed was the correct starting agent – and that was Geddes himself. Geddes's ambitions in the 1890s for stirring up in Edinburgh a Civic Renaissance indeed involved a 'whole clan of artists', both Scots and – surprisingly – French. This essay assesses three specific overtures Geddes made to French artists, each in his way representative of a vital strand in contemporary art.

Geddes and French mural decoration

Geddes's self-appointed task of promoting mural decoration was envisaged, in 1889, on a far-reaching scale: 'from brightening of the humblest sick room up to the permanent historic adornment of the greatest public buildings'. His active promotion of decorative schemes produced effects both in the public domain – from Edinburgh Royal Infirmary, University Hall and Ramsay Lodge to Glasgow City Chambers; and in the private – the decorative paintings done for his own apartment in Ramsay Garden and in those painted for his friend Henry Beveridge at Pitreavie Castle outside Dunfermline. The decorative schemes with which he was involved at Ramsay Lodge and St Giles's House, near the top of Edinburgh's Royal Mile, were intended to enhance the lives of Edinburgh university students, and he was spurred on by his belief that within a generation it would be possible to 'raise Edinburgh wellnigh to the level of Paris.'

Geddes's artistic vision was fostered in France, where he studied for several years and regularly returned. He attended the Expositions Universelles staged in Paris in 1878, 1889, and 1900, which afforded remarkable opportunities for taking stock of French and international achievements in the arts, science and technology. While there was widespread interest in Britain in public mural decoration at this period, Geddes's vision was more compatible with the situation in France.[2] There, the Third Republic, established since 1870, had extensively used mural decoration as a means to convey its Republican ideology – progressive and scientific – to a wide public. Decoration acted as education.[3] I would argue that Geddes gained specific inspiration from what he observed taking place both in Paris and in Montpellier.

During the Second Empire (1851-70) Paris had experienced what has been the called the 'biggest urban renewal project the world has ever seen'.[4] In its wake major schemes were undertaken to decorate old and new public buildings: the Panthéon (once again in 1885 transformed into a secular monument having shed its former identity as the église Sainte Geneviève), the Sorbonne, the mairies and the Hôtel de Ville. Geddes was a profound admirer of the achievements of France's pre-eminent muralist, Pierre Puvis de Chavannes, who worked on all these projects and whose first scheme for the Panthéon, inspired by the early life of Sainte Geneviève, was underway when Geddes was a student in the Latin quarter. Passing through Paris in December 1896, he and his wife Anna made it a priority to revisit the Puvis panels in the Panthéon.[5] On his 1889 visit, Geddes could not fail to be struck by Puvis's grand hemicycle mural – a painted celebration of the achievements of philosophy and poetry and the possibilities for science – whose unveiling inaugurated the opening of the New Sorbonne. In Montpellier, at whose Institut de Botanique he spent several months later that year and again in 1891, he was inspired by the work the mural artist Max Leenhardt was doing to enhance the ancient university.

In Geddes's 1889 address he accepted that Baron Haussmann's modernisation of Paris had produced disadvantages alongside the undoubted benefits of space and light. He criticised the monotony of the apartment buildings, the destruction of many town houses and gardens and resultant social exclusion. He pointed out that since Haussmann the working classes could no longer afford the rents in central Paris. This was the very reverse of what he was striving for in Edinburgh where, for a century or more, since the move of the well-to-do bourgeoisie to the New Town, the poor had been left to maunder in the dark insalubrious closes of the Old Town and Royal Mile. Geddes was determined to improve the living conditions of the Old Town, thus keeping the city centre a lively place. In support of his belief he engaged in a social experiment. Soon after his marriage to Anna Morton in 1886, the young couple moved from the elegance of Princes Street to James Court, one of the ancient closes in the Lawnmarket on the Royal Mile. His children grew up, as Norah (the eldest, born in 1887) recalled, playing on equal terms with the tenement dwellers. Subsequently they moved to the bespoke apartment within the Ramsay Garden complex commissioned from Capper and Mitchell adjacent to the Castle.

Geddes was not himself a practising artist, but he surrounded himself with practitioners, and gave his own distinctive impetus to their development. For example his pamphlets *Every Man his Own Art Critic*, his critical responses to the great painting exhibitions held in Manchester in 1887 and Glasgow in 1888, were circulated to artists of his acquaintance, among them Charles Mackie. While Geddes's tastes among his contemporaries in British art included such figure painters as Lawrence Alma-Tadema and Edward Burne-Jones, he acknowledged the superiority of the French when it came to landscape. In his view modern English landscape painting was still overly dominated by the Pre-Raphaelite influence, with its fascination with detail and bright, inharmonious colour – he cited Benjamin Leader whose *February Fill Dyke* (Birmingham City Art Gallery) featured at the Manchester exhibition – whereas French painting was rightly concerned with tonality and not afraid to sacrifice detail to overall effect.

The work of the Montpellier artist Max Leenhardt (1853-1941) which Geddes championed around 1890-1 could be said to have conformed

21 & 22. Max Leenhardt, *Une herborisation dans la garrigue*, 1890, and *Un laboratoire dans l'ancien Institut de Botanique*, 1890. Institut de Botanique, Montpellier.

to this general observation. In *Une herborisation dans la garrigue* 1890 (Fig.21) and *Un laboratoire dans l'ancien Institut de Botanique*, 1890 (Fig.22), Leenhardt's style is characterised by the muted colour and broad, harmonious tonal approach typical of contemporary French public decoration. In early 1891 Geddes invited Leenhardt to come and contribute to the mural scheme he was planning for Edinburgh University. To his Edinburgh artist colleague, Mary Rose Hill Burton, he wrote: 'I am pretty sure he won't be able to come. If he should you will like him, and learn something from him – he really is one of the best of the younger men.'[6] Somewhat forgotten today, Leenhardt, son of a wealthy protestant family, was beginning to win Salon medals for his large, broadly conceived and usually historical subjects. He and Geddes seem to have met in 1889-90 when Geddes and his family made a prolonged visit to Montpellier, doubtless at the invitation of Professor Charles Flahault (1852-1935), director of Montpellier's Institut de Botanique. In *Une herborisation dans la garrigue*, Flahault is the kneeling man with the blond beard and student 'toque'. However, as the latter made clear to his mother, it was not strictly a portrait since 'decorative painting does not allow for details.'[7] The fact that Geddes had accompanied Flahault on just such field work excursions in part explains his keen interest in Leenhardt's work.[8]

Geddes and Flahault had met as fellow botany students in Paris and in Roscoff, Brittany; their close friendship was cemented by the Geddes family's stay in Montpellier and return visit the following year. Following their first visit, Anna Geddes wrote an article for *The*

(Scottish) Art Review entitled 'Montpellier and its Ancient University' in which she sang the praises of Leenhardt's panels in Flahault's newly inaugurated Institut de Botanique:

> In the lecture-hall, decorated with stencillings, tablets commemorative of the famous botanists of the world, are two stately panels, 4 feet long, painted for the Institut and presented to it by M. Max Leenhardt, one of the most effective of the younger French artists. One of these panels represents the botanists in the field, the other in the laboratory, so showing the students that there are beauties worthy of an artist's pencil not only in a group of botanisers on the hillside, but even in the heterogeneous collection of bottles, microscopes, and other furniture of the laboratory.[9]

The article looked forward to the festivities of May 1890, when the University of Montpellier was to celebrate its sixth centenary with a grand festival incorporating a series of pageants and grand tented banquets. The occasion attracted students from all over the world. Because Patrick and Anna Geddes left before the festivities, Flahault described them in a series of letters. He thanked them for their support and reported that he had had Anna's article translated by a M. Valéry,[10] and that Max Leenhardt, inspired by the event, was preparing a commemorative decorative panel for the Aula or Central Hall of the University, in which foreign students, and the group of Scottish students in particular, would be given pride of place; a few weeks later, we learn, he was planning a further enormous decoration for the Salle des Fêtes of the Montpellier students' association.[11] Flahault's letters look back fondly on the time the Geddes family spent in Montpellier. Their presence had clearly helped him shake up to some extent the conservative habits of his compatriots. Urged on perhaps by Anna Geddes's example, some of the French women were prepared to venture out on botanical field trips alongside the men.

The evidence suggests that Leenhardt was indeed unable or unwilling to come to Edinburgh. Nevertheless I would argue that for Geddes these periods of productive collaborative Franco-Scottish activity in Montpellier proved of lasting significance, in many ways shaping his future career. First they reinforced his belief in the value of international cooperation, which in turn led to his energetic efforts to revive the ancient Scots' Colleges of Paris and Montpellier. Flahault was an enthusiastic supporter of the project but its realisation of course would take several decades more.[12] In the interim the two professors nevertheless exchanged students, as well as botanical drawings, maps and teaching notes. Second, the study of environment and plant habitat – *phytogéographie* and its sister discipline *phytosociologie* were pioneering aspects of the work being done by Flahault and his student Braun-Blanquet at Montpellier – became a central plank of Geddes's educational theory.[13] Finally the murals by Max Leenhardt for the university of Montpellier were a direct precedent and inspiration for the decorative schemes Geddes was to commission in Edinburgh over the next few years.

Charles Hodge Mackie, Paul Sérusier and the Nabis

One of the artists who became most closely involved in Geddes's schemes was Charles Hodge Mackie (1862-1920).[14] Chiefly remembered as a landscape painter and innovative printmaker, whilst working for Geddes Mackie turned his hand to decorative painting, book design and illustration, a range of activities in keeping with the spirit of continental Art Nouveau. This was no coincidence for Mackie provided for Geddes a tangible link to the Symbolist Nabi group who at the time, with the Neo-Impressionists, represented the most advanced art in France.

Mackie trained at Edinburgh's Trustees' Academy and was encouraged by Sir James Lawton Wingate (1846-1923). He was associated in the 1880s with the Scottish naturalist school and the Glasgow Boys George Henry and E.A. Hornel, often working like them in Galloway. In 1884 he won the Stuart prize and in 1888 his exhibition picture *E'ening Brings a' Hame*, a poetic pastoral scene, won considerable popularity at the Royal Scottish Academy. However his artistic development took a distinctive turn in the 1890s thanks to new contacts made in France. Indeed he was later judged to have gone astray at this period, notably by one of his Edinburgh admirers, James Caw, Director of the National Gallery of Scotland. Caw lamented the fact that Mackie, particularly in the decorative work done for Geddes, had allowed himself to be too much guided by a system and theory of colour harmony and picture-making.[15] Although Caw does not specifically cite French influence for this unfortunate deviation, it was arguably the Symbolist ideas Mackie gleaned in the Nabi circle that were to blame.

We do not know if it was Geddes who originally suggested to Mackie that he should make an extended visit to France, but it is likely he encouraged him and the experience was to have a direct impact on the work Mackie undertook for his mentor. In 1891 Mackie married Anne Walls, sister of the painter William Walls. In the spring of 1892 he and his new bride embarked on a walking tour of Normandy and Brittany, intending to pay homage at Gréville, the birth place of Millet. In the course of this tour, apparently prompted by a magazine article, they sought out the picturesque village of Huelgoat in central Brittany, renowned for its beautiful rocks and cascades. Anne Mackie later recalled that in Huelgoat 'we made our first acquaintance with the most advanced French art and artists'. She was not exaggerating, for they met and befriended the Symbolist painter Paul Sérusier (1864-1927), leader of the Nabi group and close friend and follower of Paul Gauguin. For all that it was unplanned, Mackie's meeting with Sérusier, two years his junior but his equal in talent and intellect, was a significant one. Paul Sérusier was well-educated, articulate and musical, with a philosophical and theoretical turn of mind.

That summer Sérusier had set up studio in Huelgoat, planning to stay for six months. Huelgoat's remoteness appealed more than the now increasingly crowded art colonies of the Finistère coast, Concarneau and Pont-Aven. He had arrived alone, but had since acquired a painting companion, a Dane named Clement. The son of well-to-do parents (his father directed the Houbigant perfumery), Sérusier had spent his summers in Brittany since the mid-1880s, attracted like many artists at that date by this relatively unspoilt and remote corner of France, so different, with its harsh climate and way of life, Celtic traditions and piety, from the cynical atmosphere of modern Paris. As Mackie would have been keen to communicate, an enthusiasm for things Celtic was strong in Geddes's circle too.

When Mackie met him, Sérusier still had all the zeal of the new convert. He had introduced himself to Gauguin in 1888 in Pont-Aven, where Gauguin had just completed his first truly Symbolist composition, *Vision of the Sermon, Jacob Wrestling with the Angel*. Gauguin was pleased to impress his new ideas on a young man of Sérusier's calibre. On returning to Paris Sérusier had founded the Nabi group, recruiting suitable candidates for membership among his fellow students at the Académie Julian. The formation of this secret brotherhood was Sérusier's way of sharing the important new artistic truths he had absorbed from Gauguin. Subsequently Sérusier had spent extended periods with Gauguin at Le Pouldu, on the coast of Brittany not far from Pont-Aven, before Gauguin's departure in 1891 for Tahiti.

The new credo, taken from Gauguin and preached by Sérusier, was a direct attack on the run-of-the-mill, dead-end naturalism which his generation had been taught to practise – and which, in Sérusier's case had earned him a place at the Paris Salon. His new synthetist and Symbolist style, close to that of Gauguin, is exemplified by his beautiful triptych *La Cueillette de Pommes* (Fig.23). Hardly surprisingly, the Scottish visitors were

23. Paul Sérusier, *La Cueillette de Pommes*, 1891. Triton Foundation.

24. (*Above*) Charles H. Mackie, *Breton Girl Crocheting*, 1892. Private Collection.

25. (Left to right) Paul Ranson, Paul Sérusier and France Ranson in Sérusier's studio, c.1892-3. Photo courtesy of Brigitte Ranson Bitker.

taken aback, but intrigued by Sérusier's and Clement's recent work: 'Although to us their work seemed queer, yet it had a curious fascination in spite of misshapen peasants and pink ploughed fields'.[16] They were accustomed to paintings in a tonal earthy palette; indeed Mackie probably identified quite closely with Sérusier's earlier style. But instead, he seems to have tried his hand at treating a distinctly Sérusier-like subject and using a bold, Nabiesque way of laying down colours (Fig.24).

Sérusier was no mere imitator of Gauguin. He was a persuasive teacher, soon developing theories about colour use and exploring a more subdued range of tones than the bright hues used by Gauguin. Under his tutelage the Nabis had developed a commitment to decorative values, especially to mural painting. Indeed Sérusier made the extraordinary declaration in the press in June 1892, just at the time he met Mackie: 'Paul Sérusier is abandoning the easel picture for the decoration. He has decided to cover with frescoes whatever walls are entrusted to him.'[17] His theories about colour harmony, in contrast to those of the Neo-Impressionists which were based on the breaking down of light to its optical constituents, revolved around the importance of grey in establishing the keynote for the rest of the palette. Just as he had conveyed this idea to his fellow Nabis, Ranson, Denis and Vuillard, Sérusier clearly impressed upon Mackie the importance of 'seeking out the grey', for as Anne Mackie noted, 'after making endless experiments, that simple remark became the foundation of C.H.M.'s theories'.

In Charles and Anne Mackie's collection, there were two gouache studies of a Breton servant, once thought to be by Gauguin. (His name indeed

appears on one of the sheets, although the handwriting bears no resemblance to Gauguin's.) They are in
all likelihood a direct memento of the
1892 Huelgoat encounter. The full
face study of *Louise the Servant Woman*
by Sérusier is presumably either a
study for or replica of his oil of the
same subject (1891, Saint Germain-
en-Laye, Musée Départemental
Maurice Denis, Le Prieuré.) The profile view *Paysanne bretonne de profil*
(Private Collection) (Fig.26) appears
to represent the same model.[18]

The Mackies' eventful first trip to
France came to an abrupt end in the
summer of 1892. Their return to
London in late July or early August
was precipitated by the sudden and
shocking death of Sérusier's mother
Clémence, to whom the artist was
very close.[19] Sérusier's family had
only just arrived from Paris to spend
the holidays, and they quickly got

26. Paul Sérusier, *Paysanne bretonne de profil*,
c.1891. Private Collection.

onto the friendliest of terms with the young Scottish couple staying at the
same hotel. Mme Sérusier's death was put down to a violent attack of food
poisoning or cholera, which was apparently rampant in the village. Anne
and Charles were much impressed by the midnight service in the dimly-lit
chapel which preceded the return of her body to Paris. (Perhaps at Mackie's
suggestion, Geddes's *Evergreen* would later feature an article on Breton
funeral practices.) They were accompanied on their return to London by
Sérusier's friend Clement whom Mackie was pleased to initiate into the
work of J.M.W. Turner. One suspects that Mackie's regular visits to the
National Gallery and British Museum, where he undertook copies of the
old masters, now had the renewed purpose of putting Sérusier's theories to
the test.

Anne Mackie's journal continues: 'We returned to Paris the following
May to be most hospitably received by M. Sérusier who introduced us to his
friends at a delightful luncheon party.' Although this suggests their second
trip to France began in May 1893, two pieces of internal evidence make
clear that the events of the visit she describes cannot have taken place
until 1894. It is possible that an intervening visit to France occurred in
1893 and that she confused the dates.[20] First, she refers to a meeting
which occurred at a Manet exhibition: 'He [Sérusier] also told us of an
exhibition of 40 Manets at Durand-Ruel's which was to close in two days –

a great opportunity and lasting pleasure for still after many years, his beautiful work remains in my memory. There we met Guthrie and Lavery. Lavery was a charming person to meet. Guthrie more self-conscious and aloof ... ' This exhibition, which is omitted from most of the Manet literature, took place in April-May 1894.[21] Guthrie had his own reasons to be visiting Paris at this time as he had four paintings on show at the Société Nationale des Beaux-Arts which opened on 25 April.[22] Anne Mackie goes on to describe their visit to Gauguin's studio where they were presented with his recent Tahitian work 'of beautiful colour and intensely interesting and sincere'. Again, Gauguin's presence in Paris points to the year being 1894 not 1893 when he was still in Tahiti. But the window of opportunity for their meeting was tight. He returned to Paris in September 1893, held an exhibition at Durand-Ruel's gallery in November, and at some date in early May 1894 left for Brittany. Gauguin's strange paintings, pottery and wood carvings and new, exotic subject matter had a sincerity and power that, in Anne Mackie's view, outclassed the 'affectations of his followers'.

On this 1894 visit to Paris, through Sérusier the Mackies met other members of the Nabi group: Paul Ranson, an inventive draughtsman and decorative artist, whose studio in the Boulevard Montparnasse served as their regular meeting place, and Edouard Vuillard, who took them to his studio and invited them to pick a work to take home.[23] Conscious of his impecunious state they chose the smallest they could find, according to Anne Mackie, a tiny painting on cardboard, but they chose well. Decorative in effect with patches of bold colour, and typically ambiguous in its treatment of space, *Ouvrières dans l'atelier de couture* (1893) (Fig.27) is a fine example of Vuillard's early Nabi experimentation. Happily, having been in Edinburgh for many years in the Mackies' and later in Stanley Cursiter's private collections, it is now on public view. The Nabis were enthusiastic performers of puppet plays; hospitality was freely offered and returned, Anne buttering piles of sandwiches in order to provide her new friends with a proper Scottish tea. In Ranson's spacious studio they even taught the French the rudiments of cricket! Difficulties inevitably occurred concerning the l.b.w. rule, and Charles Mackie's unfortunate translation, 'jambon devant wicket', was a slip which apparently applied all too well to Mme Ranson's 'sumptuous leg', reducing his wife to helpless laughter. If the Franco-Scottish relations were easy chez Ranson, it is harder to imagine what the high-minded Scottish couple made of Gauguin and his milieu. Anne Mackie later, apparently, forbade the men-

27. Edouard Vuillard, *Ouvrières dans l'atelier de couture*, 1893. Scottish National Gallery of Modern Art, Edinburgh.

28 & 29. Charles H. Mackie, *Spring, Felling Trees*, 1893, and *Winter, Raking Leaves*, 1893, decorative panels in Patrick Geddes's apartment, Ramsay Garden. Photo © Mike Small, SCRAN.

tion of Goethe in her hearing because he had had 'mistresses'.[24] And yet she seems to have fallen for Gauguin's charm, being taken, she recalls, 'under his wing'. Fortuitously, Gauguin's half-caste mistress of the moment, Anna the Javanese, seems not to have been in evidence.

Between the visits to France, Mackie's services, together with those of fellow artist John Duncan, were fully enlisted in Edinburgh by Patrick Geddes. Mackie undertook mural work for Ramsay Garden which he executed in a decorative, somewhat Symbolist style, quite unlike the naturalistic work he had exhibited in the 1880s. It was to the synthetic style and theory of Sérusier and the Nabis, rather than to Gauguin's work, that Charles Mackie responded. One notices similarities of theme, composition, arabesque line and unmodulated colour use when comparing Sérusier's decorative work (for instance Fig.23 and the two panels seen in the background of Fig.25) and Mackie's *Spring* and *Winter* panels painted in 1893-4 for Geddes's apartment (Figs 28, 29). His choice of subject matter – rural themes of woodcutting, gathering flowers, raking leaves – parallels Sérusier's, although

Mackie has an elegance of drawing style which differs from the French artist's wilfully primitivist forms.

For his embossed leather cover design for *The Evergreen* Mackie took as his motif a tree with spreading branches and roots, which Geddes was delighted to identify as the *arbor vitae*, or tree of life (Fig. 30).[25] The elegant arabesque design recalls the stylised linearity of Paul Ranson and contemporary Art Nouveau book bindings by the Ecole de Nancy – such artists as Camille Martin and Victor Prouvé – the quality of whose display of leather bindings at the Salon de la Société Nationale des Beaux-Arts of 1894 was noted at the time. We have seen that there is every likelihood Mackie visited that Salon.

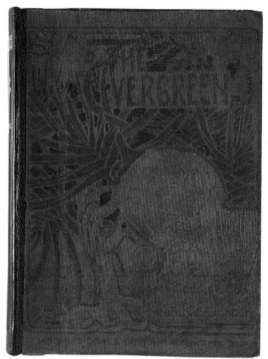

30. Charles H. Mackie, Embossed cover design with Tree of Life from *The Evergreen, The Book of Spring*, 1895. © National Library of Scotland.

Letters of 1893 and 1894 from Mackie to Geddes, apart from constantly pressing for payment, refer to this work and to the teaching he had undertaken at Geddes's behest in the School of Art – training house painters in the understanding of the harmony of colours for example. It is clear that he was charged with achieving results in terms of durability and matt effect similar to the French artists Geddes admired. At one point Mackie urges Geddes to ensure that Dott – his picture framer – when fixing these new panels in situ 'does not go all over them with his bare paws but puts smooth paper between the panel and his hand when pressing them down. Under other circumstances the natural grease of his hand might be an excellent and cheap form of varnishing but one scarcely of advantage to preserving the bloom of a dead surfaced wall painting.'[26] This search for a matt effect is another link to Nabi decoration – indeed varnish was totally abhorred by Sérusier. In a letter of early 1894, written shortly before he was to return to Paris, Mackie reassures Geddes that the care he is taking over his choice of canvas and its preparation will ensure the panels' durability. 'All French decorators use absorbent canvas much more slightly prepared than this of mine. I have no doubt that generations yet unborn will see these panels as you see them.'[27] And he assures Geddes that the panels of Autumn and Spring pastorals destined for what he calls 'Allan Ramsay's Room' should be in position by 13 April.

Mackie kept in touch with his new French friends, well aware of the similarities between the decorative aims of the Geddesian group and theirs. It was Mackie who persuaded Geddes to invite Sérusier to Edinburgh in the summer of 1894 to participate in the cultural renewal taking place there: his letter of May 1894 refers to this eventuality.[28] He ends the letter by giving his patron Sérusier's Paris address but warning that he does not think he is 'available for summer work'. He advises, with some caution, 'I don't care to be responsible in any way for the introduction of his work as it might not give satisfaction to most people.' Equally Sérusier's reply to the professor's invitation shows a certain ambivalence.[29] He was not keen to undertake any teaching duties although he would welcome the chance to paint mural decorations or to find an outlet for tapestry work. Unfortunately we cannot tell whether he ever followed up this unexpected opportunity; we only know that he submitted his illustration, *Pastorale bretonne* (Fig.44) to the Spring number of *The Evergreen*. The fact that there are no further mentions of Sérusier in an Edinburgh context, and that he spent that summer, having just fallen in love, in the company of a Polish woman, Gabriella Zapolska, suggests he declined.[30] Journeying to Scotland, however attractive, was an expensive undertaking for a young artist, as Lucien Pissarro would later point out to his father. Surprisingly, it seems not to have been

31. Charles H. Mackie, *Lyart Leaves* from *The Evergreen, The Book of Autumn*, 1895, p.19.

Sérusier, as has previously been supposed, who was responsible for *The Evergreen* winning a subscriber by the name of Mme A. Henry in Pont-Aven. The person responsible for the contact was Augustin Hamon.[31]

Although there is no evidence that Mackie kept up contact with Sérusier, he seems to have wanted to stay in touch with the Ransons, inscribing them a friendly New Year greeting when he sent copies of his *Evergreen* woodcuts *Lyart Leaves* (Fig.31) and *Hide and Seek*. The graphic styles cultivated by the two artists have marked similarities when one compares these woodcuts with Ranson's pen and ink sketch of Huelgoat, a record of a visit to Sérusier in 1893. Ranson was a versatile artist, showing considerable talents in the design of wallpaper, stained glass and tapestries woven by his wife France and inspired, in this instance, by his beautiful sister-in-law

32. Paul Ranson, *Moisson fleurie*, lost stained glass window executed in Tiffany glass and designed for Siegfried Bing, 1895, as reproduced in *The Magazine of Art*, March 1897. © National Library of Scotland.

Germaine. It was to France Ranson, nicknamed by the Nabis the 'Lumière du Temple', that Mackie dedicated his copy of Botticelli's *Nativity*. An abiding puzzle that lingers from their contacts is the disappearance, into a Scottish collection perhaps, of Ranson's wonderful stained glass window, *Moisson fleurie* (Fig. 32), following its exhibition in Edinburgh in 1900.

Doubtless impressed by the success of the Ramsay Garden project, Henry Beveridge, a linen manufacturer and friend of Geddes, offered both Mackie and John Duncan the job of painting decorative panels in his Dunfermline home, Pitreavie Castle. Fortunately these were described at the time in an article by Margaret Armour in *The Studio*, as today, sadly, the only trace of their existence is a few sketches. Armour praised Mackie's 'individual and distinguished' style, commenting that at Pitreavie his work showed a 'growth in ornamental treatment. The figures are unmistakably conventionalised, but so artfully as hardly to seem wrested at all from their natural forms; and the composition [based on the *Ballad of Sir Patrick Spens*], though rigidly decorative, is alive with old-world romance.' [32]

The ways in which Mackie broke from Scottish conventions in his decorative work for Geddes and Beveridge in the 1890s, together with his subsequent experimentation with colour printing in the 1900s, in which medium he was to prove highly innovative, must to some extent be attributable to his formative encounters with the Nabi group and to their belief in the priority of the decorative arrangement of forms and colours on a flat surface.

Augustin Hamon and Lucien Pissarro

The third French artist who was almost drawn into the Geddes circle was Lucien Pissarro. Eldest son of the Impressionist painter, Lucien Pissarro (1863-1944) acted as an important conduit for Franco-British artistic ideas at the end of the 19th century. His background was entirely French: he had grown up surrounded by the Impressionists and witnessing his father Camille's struggles for recognition as a painter in Paris. In 1883 he moved temporarily to London, and in 1890, together with his younger brother Georges who was apprenticed as a furniture maker to C.R. Ashbee, he established himself there permanently, quickly becoming assimilated into advanced art circles. Having developed as an Impressionist and then converted to neo-Impressionist divisionism, Lucien embarked in England upon an independent career as a wood engraver, playing an influential role in this ancient medium's revival in the 1890s. He quickly became involved with the Arts and Crafts movement led by William Morris, although his father Camille was suspicious of its Pre-Raphaelite and Symbolist overtones. Lucien became a friend and collaborator of Charles Ricketts and Charles Shannon and, from 1893 on, exhibited with the Arts and Crafts Society. With Ricketts, Lucien produced a treatise on typography. He also got to know an associate of Geddes, the bookbinder T.J. Cobden-Sanderson (1840-1922), co-founder with Morris of the Arts and Crafts Exhibition Society, famous for his Doves Bindery in Hammersmith. Cobden-Sanderson was also Secretary of the English branch of the New Brussels University, which may explain his close involvement with the Reclus family.

Once Lucien Pissarro came to his attention there were thus many reasons for Geddes to have been interested in his work, and vice versa. The specific link was provided by Augustin Hamon. As Siân Reynolds' essay explains, at the time of his visit to Edinburgh Hamon was essentially on the run from France, his writings on anarchism making him look like an *agent provocateur*. He was in close contact with the Pissarros, father and son, who were non-violent sympathisers of the anarchist cause, but it was Cobden-Sanderson and Paul Reclus who suggested that he apply to Geddes for a room at University Hall in January 1895. Hamon was welcomed by Geddes, and he soon found himself engaged to deliver a series of lectures on 'La France actuelle' at Geddes's 1895 Summer Meeting. During his winter stay in Edinburgh, Hamon took a personal interest in the talented artists surrounding Geddes, particularly Mackie and Duncan.[33] In a letter to his friend Lucien, who on Hamon's suggestion had just sent a series of his woodcuts to the Scottish artists, he gave an enthusiastic description of their work. Indeed Hamon's letters to Lucien are highly informative about the range and intensity of Geddesian artistic activity in early 1895. For example he pointed out that John Duncan, despite speaking no French, 'knows French painting and the Impressionists' work, for instance Camille Pissarro's ...' He continued:

> Around Geddes there is a whole clan of artists. And your prints gave so much pleasure that they all wanted to have one. The result was that Duncan ended up with none and I'm counting on you to send him a second copy of the young girl alone, a beautiful woodcut. He prefers that to the others. The little girls dancing became the property of C.H. Mackie, ... a painter aged 32, an original landscapist constantly researching new techniques; he has talent, much talent perhaps. In any case he is not banal. He has been in France. At the moment he is doing zincographs, experimenting with colour impressions for a book 'New Evergreen' which University Hall is going to publish termly, like the Yellow Book. It is Geddes who has organised this New Evergreen and he has asked me to write an article

for the Summer number. In the Spring number there is going to be a drawing by Séruzier [sic] whom you perhaps know. He's a friend of Mackie.

The drawing of the woman alone went to Brown Macdougall a young draughtsman who lives with Duncan in Riddle's Court, University Hall. Macdougall is working on views of the city for a feature in Studio and he is preparing a volume of illustrations on Edinburgh. He likes to draw caricatures and in those he takes some of his inspiration from Caran d'Ache. For ornamental drawing he recalls Walter Crane. He hasn't much originality but plenty of verve.

Also at University Hall but not at Riddle's Court there are MM. Cadenhead Smith and Burn Murdoch, painters; M. Finlayson who is a craftsman, sculptor and modeller; and some young ladies including Duncan's pupils.

I've given your address to Duncan, Macdougall and Mackie. I discussed as well an exhibition of French painters; I think that will be possible perhaps next year. What is needed is to keep up friendly relations with all these young people who, like us, are full of ardour and enthusiasm. I think that collaborating on N. Everg. with a drawing would help to cement these links of international but professional solidarity.'[34]

From the date and brief descriptions it is possible to propose which of his recent woodcuts Lucien sent, eager to publicise his newly established press (Fig. 33).[35] And it is easy to see why the Scots artists would have been enthusiastic for they combine the charm and simplification of Nabi art with a high level of English craftsmanship. There seems little question that they were of tangible influence on the woodcuts Mackie designed for The Evergreen (Fig. 34). Lucien for his part was certainly keen to make closer contact with the Geddes group. 'Hamon has put me in touch with some Scots from Edinburgh,' he wrote to his father, 'who liked my wood engravings and are familiar with your painting, they are University people, I must try to see about organising an exhibition. If at a given moment I can go there, I could establish relations, which could prove useful one day.'[36] Sadly lack of funds on both sides meant Lucien Pissarro was unable to get to Edinburgh and the exciting idea of mounting an exhibition of Neo-Impressonist painting in Edinburgh was never realised.[37]

33. Lucien Pissarro, La Ronde, 1893, Ashmolean Museum, Oxford.

34. Charles H. Mackie, *When the Girls Come Out to Play* from *The Evergreen, The Book of Spring*, 1895, p.67. © National Library of Scotland.

At the time of Hamon's visit and observations of the artistic scene in Edinburgh in 1895 – a time when Glasgow too was at the height of its cultural expansion – the opportunities for Franco-Scottish artistic exchange seemed boundless. But what became of the synergy Geddes had so successfully created among his group? Why was it not sustained? A number of possible reasons can be given, the most obvious of which is that the money ran out for the decorative schemes, and several artists who had patiently awaited their payments were disappointed. Geddes was never a scrupulous keeper of accounts and his correspondence, not just with artists but with the many others whose contributions to his schemes he had encouraged, reveals this as a continuing worry. Geddes was probably relieved of a sense of unfulfilled obligation towards John Duncan when in 1900, through his contacts with Jane Addams and others, he secured him a teaching position in Chicago's Parker School.

Charles Mackie, perhaps less dependent on Geddes from the outset than Duncan, increasingly went his own way, reverting to the easel paintings that had initially won him clients. He travelled in France and Italy, and became known for his sensitive Whistlerian crepuscular Venetian themes. He also concentrated on the woodcut, perfecting an idiosyncratic technique which produced remarkably rich results. He explained his procedure in an article for *The Studio*: 'I have discarded the key-block entirely and I rely for my effects on colour-shapes carefully juxtaposed. I use seven or eight oak blocks for each print, and do not limit myself as to the number of times I may lay the print on each block. Briefly, I might describe it as an emotional use of the printing-press, differing from painting only in block-shapes being used instead of brush marks.'[38] While his fondness for French rural motifs was common enough among British artists at the period, his readiness to play with abstract forms, experiment with print techniques and theorise about colour were exceptional, a lasting legacy, one might argue, of Mackie's close encounters with the Nabis in the early 1890s. His distinguished pupil Laura Knight, with whom he founded the Staithes Art Club, remembered his teaching and advice about colour throughout her career.

Postscript: Geddes in Montpellier, 1924-32

Although his activities during the Exposition Universelle in Paris in 1900 were an extension of the Edinburgh Summer Meetings, Geddes's remarkable commitment to the arts flagged somewhat from this date on. He was sidetracked by new passions: in the later 1890s the humanitarian crisis in Armenia drew him to make a botanical survey of Cyprus which he envis-

35. Collège des Ecossais, Montpellier, 1928. Photo © National Library of Scotland.

aged as a potential refuge. Thenceforth his prime energies would be directed towards town planning, and this meant being increasingly drawn away from Edinburgh – proselytising for the ideas which he had partially realised in his native capital. When invited to draw up a plan for Dunfermline – an idea first mooted in a letter from John Ross of 1895 – by the steel magnate and philanthropist Andrew Carnegie, cultural institutes played a central role in his concept. But the plan, published in 1904, was never realised. His lasting contribution to Edinburgh, in addition to the Ramsay Garden complex and the Outlook Tower, was the landscaping of Edinburgh zoo. In later years Geddes was active in India and Israel, drawing up the plans for Bombay and Jerusalem universities.

Eventually Geddes was forced to curtail his ceaseless travelling and international activity. Diminished by the death of his wife Anna and son Alasdair during the First World War, he returned to Europe and decided to settle in Montpellier, where he had spent such a happy and fruitful time as a young man. There at last he was able to realise the unfulfilled project of 1890 which his old friend Charles Flahaut had attempted to keep alive: the Collège des Ecossais (Fig.35).[39] Established on the northern fringes of the city it stands to this day, a strange amalgam of Languedoc *mas* and Scottish tower house, incorporating its own outlook tower to match that of Edinburgh, with views southwards over the roofs of the city to the Mediterranean sea and northwards over vines and garrigue to the foothills of the Cévennes. Geddes's younger son Arthur carved Geddesian motifs, including the motto *Vivendo discimus* (By living we learn) into the walls, and Geddes, practising Voltaire's famous dictum, cultivated his garden, planting the terraces with native specimens and creating shady walks. The purpose of the Collège des Ecossais, and of the Collège des Indiens established alongside it, was to enable Scottish and other foreign students to study abroad, as Geddes himself had done, by offering them a congenial ambience, a home from home. He was committed to establishing the same kind of stimulating international and intellectual exchange that had characterised Edinburgh in the 1890s. With its historic botanical garden, ancient university and medical school, Montpellier offered, in Geddes's view, manifold advantages as a place to begin assimilating Western culture. They were similar qualities to those of Edinburgh in terms of manageability of scale, geographical situation between mountain and sea and richness and visibility of cultural history; in addition, Montpellier had a considerably more benign climate.[40]

The Collège des Ecossais project turned out to be Geddes's ultimate endeavour: he died in Montpellier and his funeral oration was read by his old friend Charles Flahault. In this renewal of his close ties with France, in some ways Geddes's life came full circle and at his death he could rely on his work being carried forward, in the short term at least, by his old friend Paul Reclus. Sadly the Collège fell into disuse in the 1950s and although there have been ideas of reviving it as a multi-disciplinary environmental planning centre, these remain on the drawing board.

Geddes believed passionately in the benefits to be gained from international and, in particular, from Franco-Scottish exchange. Over the last half-century, some at least of his ambitions for Edinburgh as a European city of culture have surely been realised in the annual summer Festival. And his vision on the artistic front in the 1890s had immense potential. His enthusiasm and wide range of connections drew him to three French artists of quality and innovation. Had the links been followed through, had Geddes's schemes met with greater support in Edinburgh, his vision of a Scots cultural renaissance might have been more completely achieved.

NOTES

* 'Around Geddes there's a whole clan of artists ... What we need to do ... is maintain friendly relations with all these young people who, like us, are full of ardour and enthusiasm.'

1. P. Geddes, 'On national and municipal encouragement of art upon the Continent', in *Transactions of the National Association for the Advancement of Art* 1889, pp.297-308

2. See Willsdon, *Mural Painting*.

3. For a recent exploration of Puvis de Chavannes' murals in their ideological context see J. Shaw, *Dream States, Puvis de Chavannes, Modernism and the Fantasy of France*, New Haven & London, 2002.

4. Anthony Sutcliffe, *Paris, An Architectural History*, New Haven & London, 1993, p.83.

5. A letter dated 10 December 1896 from Anna Geddes in Paris to her children at home enthusiastically describes the Puvis murals and encourages them to seek out reproductions of his work in the Outlook Tower (NLS Ms 19994). That same year a specially-commissioned lithographed poster by Auguste Lauzet of Puvis's Ste Geneviève murals had been pasted onto hoardings in the boulevard des Capucines, a moralising initiative of Geddes's friend Paul Desjardins and his Union pour l'Action Morale. Under the Union's aegis a reduced version was also circulated. The poster-sized prints were published by Patrick Geddes & Colleagues as part of the Ethic Art Series, and these must be the reproductions in the Outlook Tower to which Anna Geddes refers. See Fowle, p.39 below.

6. Geddes to Mary Rose Hill Burton, from Nice, 28 February 1891 (NLS Ms 10508A, f.52).

7. Unpublished letter from Charles Flahault to his mother of 7 March 1890, courtesy Jean-Marie Emberger.

8. The pair of Leenhardt panels have long since been removed from their original decorative setting and now hang on a landing of Montpellier's 1950s Institut de Botanique.

9. Anna Geddes, 'Montpellier and its ancient university', p.132, in *(Scottish) Art Review*, Vol.3, 1890, pp.130-4. Flahault arranged for it to be translated (see n.10).

10. At one such banquet the 19-year-old Paul Valéry, a Montpellier law student and as yet unknown as a poet, met the poet Pierre Louÿs, a significant encounter as it was through Louÿs that he would soon afterwards meet André Gide. The French translator of Anna Geddes's article is more likely to have been Valéry's elder brother Jules (1863-1938), who was also a law student and later professor of law at Montpellier University and is presumably the 'Montpellier friend' referred to in a letter of 1930 from Thomas Barclay to Patrick Geddes. See Fraser (ed.), *Geddes Tagore Correspondence*, p.148. I am grateful to Brian Stimpson for information about Valéry's family.

11. Flahault to Geddes, 1 juin 1890, T.GED 12/3/2 and 19 juillet 1890, T.GED 12/3/2. One of the large decorations mentioned by Flahault, *Réception du Président Sadi Carnot à l'Université de Montpellier*, is currently in storage in Montpellier. I am grateful to Victor Pellegrin for supplying information about Leenhardt.

12. Flahault's letter of 29 mai 1890 ends with a rapturous: 'Vive le collège des Ecossais! Vivent Mr. et Mme Geddes. Vivent la France et l'Université de Montpellier!' (T.GED 12/3/2).

13. A new plant classification system according to habitat was developed in Montpellier by Braun-Blanquet. I am grateful for this information to Henry Naulty of the Royal Botanic Garden, Edinburgh, and to Marie-France Flahault and J.-M. Emberger for information concerning Charles Flahault.

14. I am most grateful to W.B.C. Mackie for sharing with me the fruits of his detailed research into the life of his great uncle.

15. Caw, *Scottish Painting*, p.424.

16. Anne Mackie's Journal is a retrospective account written probably in the 1920s of the couple's adventures and meetings in France (NLS Acc 9177). Extracts from this document were published in Hardie, *Scottish Painting*, pp.121-3.

17. 'Paul Séruzier [sic] abandonne le *tableau* pour la *décoration*. Il est décidé à couvrir de fresques tous les murs qu'on lui confiera.' A. Aurier, 'Choses d'art', *Mercure de France*, June 1892, p.186.

18. Given by Anne Mackie, some time after her husband's death, to Stanley Cursiter, then Director of the National Gallery of Scotland, who still believed them to be by Gauguin, in 1976. The two works were offered for sale as Sérusiers at Christie's London on 24 June 1986 and 1 Dec. 1987. Guicheteau in his catalogue raisonné dates *Paysanne bretonne*, its verso *Paysans dansant* and *Louise ou la servante bretonne* to 1890. Marcel Guicheteau, *Paul Sérusier*, tome II, Pontoise 1989, pp.87-8, cat. nos 27, 28, 29. The author prefers 1891 given the Huelgoat setting.

19. From other sources we know this death to have occurred on 18 July 1892. See *Nabis 1888-1900*, exh. cat. Zurich, Kunsthaus, Paris, Galeries Nationales du Grand Palais, 1993, p.481.

20. In a letter to Professor Geddes dated 26 October 1893 (Strathclyde University Archives T.GED 9/76 & T.GED 9/78), Mackie expresses regret that the Geddes's last holiday – which was also a walking tour – did not coincide with their own, which could suggest that both couples were in France again in 1893.

21. Letter to the author dated 9 July 1998 from Caroline Durand-Ruel Godfroy, archivist at the Durand-Ruel Galleries, '... une exposition Manet a bien eu lieu en Avril-Mai 1894 chez nous à Paris mais ... aucun catalogue n'a été édité à cette occasion.' C. Mauclair's review of the exhibition was published in *The Art Journal*, 1895, pp.274-9.

22. I am grateful for this information to Nicola Ireland. Guthrie showed four works in the painting section, including his celebrated *En pleine été* (Royal Scottish Academy), Nos 579-82. See Gaïte Dugnat, *Les Catalogues des Salons de la Société Nationale des Beaux-Arts*, Paris 2000, Vol.1, 1890-5, p.281.

23. While the Mackies may have met other Nabis such as Maurice Denis, I have found no evidence to suggest that they were particularly close or in communication, as is claimed in Julian Halsby, *Scottish Watercolours 1740-1940*, 1986, p.192 (information repeated in the exhibition catalogue *Charles Hodge Mackie*, Bourne Fine Art, April-May 1988).

24. Private communication, courtesy W.B.C. Mackie.

25. Patrick Geddes to Charles Mackie, 4 Feb. 1895, 'Of all the plants in the Universe you have chosen the one which for evolutionary purposes pleases me best, and I cannot tell you how happy an omen it is for the scientific side of the undertaking. (Mr. Thomson and I are prepared to prove that this was the original *arbor vitae* itself, and have already adopted it for the modern symbol of evolution – genealogical tree of living species!) I take it as an omen that Science and Art are going to be better friends than ever. Of course you will notice the forking stem habit

of this plant. – *Aloe plicatilis* is its technical name.' NLS Ms10508A, f.94.

26. Letter to Professor Geddes dated October 15, 1893 (Strathclyde University Archives, T.GED 9/76).

27. Letter of early 1894 (March?),Strathclyde University Archives (T.GED 9/2173).

28. Clare Willsdon was the first person to draw attention to this proposal. See her article 'Paul Sérusier the Celt', pp.88-91.

29. Sérusier's letter to Mackie, communicated by the latter to Geddes, is in the Strathclyde University Archives (T.GED 9/2280).

30. Willsdon, *Mural Painting*, p.326 leaves the possibility open.

31. Letter in English to Geddes on headed notepaper, 5.X.95, Hotel Gloanec, Pont-Aven, Finistère, France, from Mme A. Henry (NLS Ms10527, f.223). Her knowledge of *The Evergreen* evidently came through her friend Hamon (see n.33), himself a Breton, rather than through Sérusier. Nor was she connected with the innkeeper Marie Henry at Le Pouldu, as Clare Willsdon (n.28) suggests, p.90.

32. Margaret Armour, 'Mural decoration in Scotland, Part I', *Studio*, Vol.10, Feb. 1897, p.106. Confusingly, Armour refers to Beveridge by the first name of James.

33. Augustin Hamon (1862-1945) was a man of many parts, formerly an engineer and now an active writer on social and political issues. His close association with the anarchist movement, many of whose leading lights had been arrested in a sweeping round-up in 1894, explains his seeking refuge abroad. See Reynolds, pp.75-6 below further details.

34. Augustin Hamon to Lucien Pissarro, 3 February 1895, unpublished, Pissarro archive, Ashmolean Museum, Oxford.

35. In 1894 Lucien Pissarro established the Eragny Press, named after the village in the Oise where his father lived. The vogue for woodcut in the 1890s, evident also in the work of Mackie and Gauguin, came about as a reaction to the mechanised reproductive methods used in mass-circulation illustrated journals of the day.

36. Lucien Pissarro to Camille Pissarro, 14 February 1895: 'Hamon m'a mis en relations avec des Ecossais d'Edinburgh, qui ont aimé mes gravures et qui connaissent ta peinture, ce sont des gens de l'Université, il va falloir que je tache de voir pour une exposition – Si à un moment donné je puis aller là-bas, je pourrai nouer des relations, qui pourront être utile un jour.' From Anne Thorold (ed.), *The Letters of Lucien to Camille Pissarro, 1883-1903*, Cambridge University Press 1993, p.405.

37. It would seem that financial considerations were a major obstacle to Lucien Pissarro's following up his contacts with the Geddes circle. In a letter of 22 April 1898 Lucien wrote to clear up a misunderstanding on his father's part: 'Qui diable t'as dit que j'allais en Ecosse? Il faut être calé pour y aller, comme dit Maufra ...' 'Who the devil told you I was going to Scotland? You have to be well-heeled to go there, as Maufra says ...' Thorold (n.36), p.566.

38. Quoted from 'Wood-engraving for colour', *Studio*, Vol.58, 1913, p.296.

39. Charles Flahault's letter to Geddes dated 5 June 1891 was written on the headed notepaper of the 'Comité de Patronage des étudiants étrangers à Montpellier' which he had recently formed with Geddes's support (NLS Ms10525, f.104).

40. Elisée Reclus had argued that the Mediterranean region, geographically at the crossroads, united by Latin culture, was the context in which the anarchists' utopian dream of decentralisation and of universal brotherhood stood the greatest chance of success. See A. Dymond, 'A politicized pastoral: Signac and the cultural geography of Mediterranean France', *Art Bulletin*, Vol.85, No.2, June 2003, pp.353-70.

IV. Patrick Geddes's French Connections in Academic and Political Life: Networking from 1878 to the 1900s

SIÂN REYNOLDS

Patrick Geddes is a figure of Protean variety. As Murdo Macdonald puts it, 'at first glance he is seen nowhere; but with a little digging, he's hard to miss'.[1] But in some respects he fits the French term 'intellectuel', a word coined in the 1890s, in the context of the famous Dreyfus Affair: it referred to those who lived by the intellect but who applied it to a wider world than the academy – often by taking a public stance on matters of principle. This is perhaps no accident, in view of Geddes's many wide-ranging contacts with France during his most formative years.

This essay examines Geddes's connections to major figures in French public and intellectual life over the last two decades of the 19th century. How did a Scottish outsider manage to mobilise certain pre-existing French networks, resulting in a remarkable degree of international contact? His activities have passed comparatively unobserved, both from the French and the Scottish side, yet with only a little exaggeration, it can be argued that the Geddes networks had links to the later diplomatic *entente cordiale* of 1904, and they certainly had an impact on the international exchange of ideas.

Networking, as it would be called today, can take many shapes. A network may be endogenous, that is, formed between people who share a location and background from the start, or exogenous, linking people from different backgrounds. It may be 'ego-centric', attached to a central figure, or socio-centric, focused on an idea or a group. A network can be formed gradually and coherently, or haphazardly and accidentally. It may emerge for a clear purpose, or for none – and so on. The Geddesian networks in both Scotland and France appear, like their inspirer, to fit almost every category. They seem to shift from informal and affectionate links, made by a man already charismatic in his student days, into a series of target-oriented groups. They crossed frontiers and were often attached to projects which were inspirational if not always easy to realise.

To discover Geddes's French networks means moving outwards from Geddes's biography (in its various versions), his correspondence and papers, tracing several clusters of people and their connections. In this essay, they will be described under key category headings, but in broadly chronological order.[2]

Academic contacts: natural science and social science

Geddes's first link with France was a scientific one. In the summer of 1878, aged twenty-four, having studied science in London with T.H. Huxley, Geddes went as a student of marine biology to the field station at Roscoff, Brittany. He was made welcome there by Henry de Lacaze-Duthiers of the Sorbonne.[3] Friends made at Roscoff led him to visit Paris, where he went to the 1878 Exhibition, listened to Louis Pasteur's lectures, and became a convert to the French capital:

> Our true University is thus in the City – nay more it is the City, great Paris herself. She is ever stretching out for us her fresh ideas, in the bright conversations of the salon and of the café and so she diffuses them into the intellectual atmosphere and at every social level.[4]

(Perhaps a rather optimistic view of the diffusion of knowledge in France!) Science was at any rate the context for the first set of links, and Pasteur himself was drawn into a later Geddesian project. In the 1880s, Lacaze-Duthiers wrote to Geddes, saying: 'Your research activity ... your knowledge of histology and physiology make me think you have a brilliant future. Be a professor and come to Roscoff and Banyuls with a legion of young naturalists.'[5] Geddes did not in the end take this advice. His scientific training was unconventional, although in the 1880s he did lecture in Edinburgh. When he finally became a professor of botany at Dundee in 1889, it was with a private endowment and on special terms – leaving him free much of the year. But he maintained his links not only with Lacaze-Duthiers, but also with Professor Charles Flahault in Montpellier (Fig.37),

36. Patrick Geddes and a group of student botanists from the University of Dundee, 1892. Geddes is second from right, Anna kneeling in centre. The baby is probably Alasdair, born 1891. SCRAN, Courtesy University of Dundee Archive Services.

37. Charles Flahault, c.1892. Photo courtesy of Marie-France Flahault.

an expert on the distribution of vegetation, with whom he developed a close friendship and to whom he sent many Scottish students, including A.J. Herbertson.[6]

Passionate about the exchange of academic ideas across frontiers, Geddes was for several years instrumental both in sending science students abroad and in setting up exchange mechanisms to care for them, in Paris and in Montpellier, which he visited with his family and where he developed life-long friendships. To jump forward a few years, in 1890, Geddes's wife Anna wrote an article describing the 600th anniversary of Montpellier University, when several of Geddes's students (though not, it seems, Geddes himself) were present for the ceremonies. That year, Charles Flahault set up a welfare committee for foreign students, an informal interdisciplinary group, and encouraged Geddes's plans for a 'Scots college' there, something which came to fruition only much later. It was through Flahault that Geddes first met the historian Ernest Lavisse and the economist Charles Gide, both based in Montpellier in 1890, thus enlarging his academic contacts beyond the sciences.[7]

In the meantime, the scientific network had also led, almost accidentally, to other things. During the winter of 1878, while working on a botanical survey in Paris, Geddes dropped into a lecture at the Sorbonne given by a young man of his own age Edmond Demolins (1852-1907) a disciple of the social observer and theorist Frédéric Le Play. He was immediately inspired by certain of Le Play's ideas and observations of society, which he later combined with the philosophy of Auguste Comte, encountered at almost the same time. The subject is too large to explore here, but essentially what Geddes borrowed from Le Play was the need for a thorough sociological survey of a region, which became one of his key preoccupations, while in Comte he found the concept of the hierarchical structure of knowledge.[8] He became friendly with Demolins, and eventually a network of Le Play disciples found its way to Edinburgh. This is the 'second Geddes–France network', one passionately concerned with the social sciences.

For most of the 1880s, Geddes was taken up with his various schemes in Edinburgh, and travelled to France only from time to time. His most notable visit was for the 1889 Exhibition, commemorating the centenary of the French Revolution, when he renewed many of his contacts and extended them into some pioneering pedagogical projects, with exchanges both of students and teachers. For some years, he had been giving summer school instruction to local teachers at Granton marine biology station on the Forth. This was the time of the University extension movement both in France and Britain, under different names: extra-mural education, *universités populaires*. In the late 1880s, Geddes launched what became known as the Edinburgh Summer Meetings, a kind of summer school which functioned for more than a decade. At their peak in 1893-5, the Meetings attracted about 150 students, but always had a solid core of regular attenders, many

38. Summer meeting participants, Teviot Row House, c.1892. Photo ©
Strathclyde University Archives.

of them teachers, from a wide geographical radius (Figs 2, 4, 38). It was
during the early years that they were at their most inspirational. Geddes
invited both his scientific and his sociological contacts over from France,
eliciting a remarkable response (see names in appendix, p.80). Demolins in
particular came over in 1892, 1893 and 1895, and in his letters and
articles has left a striking record of the illumination his visits brought
him.[9]

The arrangements for tuition at the Summer Meetings were informal,
mixing the sexes – to an extent that surprised a French observer. And they
were pedagogically avant-garde and progressive, with no fixed syllabus or
exams – another surprise for those used to French education. Much stress
was placed on field work and environmental studies. Demolins brought
fellow-Le Playists over to teach/learn there too, including the Abbé Felix
Klein, Jules Bailhache, and possibly Paul de Rousiers. It was in Edinburgh
that Demolins first met Cecil Reddie, headmaster of the progressive English
school Abbotsholme, and through him the head of Bedales. The impact of
these encounters resulted in Demolins's famous book on British education,
A quoi tient la supériorité des Anglo-Saxons? ('How are we to explain the
superiority of the Anglo-Saxons?' – i.e. the British) published in 1897. This

book, with a title rather unwelcome in France, characterised British education as child-centred, character-building, and non-directive – a view more influenced by the avant-garde than the norm, perhaps. But Demolins put his money where his mouth was, and inspired the foundation of the private progressive school the Ecole des Roches in 1899 in Normandy. One of the first subscribers to the school was Jules Siegfried, a key player in the Musée Social network in Paris. The newly-founded Musée Social was an important French 'think-tank on social affairs', as it would be called now. Geddes already knew several of the individual members of this influential institution, which still exists. It was a centre for eminent philanthropists and social thinkers, and he thus had access to a new network of social science, in particular through Mlle Dick May (Jeanne Weill), the energetic secretary of the Collège Libre des Sciences Sociales.[10]

The Edinburgh Summer Meetings allowed a varied group of people to meet in the kind of circumstances that encourage rapid and intense acquaintance. One observer wrote that 20% of the participants were from abroad, so the Summer Meetings 'are better known in Paris than in London'.[11] Of the French participants, alongside the Le Playists, there were regular French academics, such as Alfred Espinas, professor of literature at Bordeaux and later the Sorbonne, and the moral philosopher Paul Desjardins. (Desjardins later organised the famous 'Décades de Pontigny' at an abbey in Burgundy, between 1910 and 1939. It may not be too fanciful to regard these ten-day meetings, bringing together writers and intellectuals, as having been inspired by Geddes's Summer Meetings). In the 1890s, a new recruit along with several others was Léon Marillier, specialist in the history of religion and adopted stepson of the leading French historian Charles Seignobos. While the Scottish colleagues whom Geddes invited to teach included several women, virtually all the French visitors, with the exception of Marie Bonnet of Montpellier, were men (unsurprisingly, given the structure of the French universities at the time).

The anarchist connection

It may seem odd that Geddes, a radical in social and cultural respects, but one who steered clear of official politics as much as he could, should have become closely linked to some celebrated French anarchists, at a time when anarchism was in the headlines. The early 1890s saw an outbreak of terrorist scares in France perpetrated by people claiming to be anarchists – including a home-made bomb thrown into the French Assemblée Nationale, and the assassination of the French President in 1894. Repressive measures were introduced against anyone connected to the anarchist movement. Geddes ended up sheltering one political anarchist from the French authorities under a false name, after some of these incidents, and was on close terms with others. It should be stressed that none of his contacts sanctioned violence, but they were still subject to arrest and pursuit by

the authorities in more than one country, for their views. How did this 'anarchist' network come about? Probably through the international scholarship of geography.

Geddes already knew Pierre Kropotkin, the famous Russian geographer and anarchist, resident in France. Kropotkin visited Edinburgh in 1886 after his release from the French prison of Clairvaux, and wrote to his friend, fellow-geographer, and fellow-anarchist Elisée Reclus afterwards, praising Geddes's installation in the Old Town and his social work with students.[12] Geddes was already an admirer of Reclus (1830-1905) (Fig.39). It seems that he simply wrote to him, possibly mentioning Kropotkin's name, in the early 1890s, inviting him to come and lecture in Edinburgh. Reclus was world-famous for his pioneer works on environmental geography, which are rather neglected today, e.g. *La Géographie Universelle*. By the 1890s, he was living and teaching in Brussels, at a privately-financed university, having been refused an official post. In his sixties but spry, he came to the Edinburgh Summer Meetings in 1893 and 1895 (walking up Arthur's Seat on one of these occasions). On16 August 1895, Reclus wrote to his wife:

In a few minutes I am going to give my second lecture. The first [geography] went off very well, before a sympathetic audience, made up of people who really seemed to understand French. My fourth lecture will have to be in English, and will be for an audience mostly made up of anarchist workmen. This will be the difficult part of the campaign.

Reclus also remarks that he has met the Le Playist Abbé Klein, who 'would like to become an anarchist but does not dare'.[13]

39. (*Above*) Elisée Reclus. Photo courtesy of Ashmolean Museum, Oxford.

40. Paul Reclus (left) and Patrick Geddes outside the Collège des Ecossais, Montpellier, c.1928. Photo courtesy of Claire Geddes.

It was presumably as a result of the close friendship between Reclus and Geddes, who admired each other's achievements, that Reclus's nephew Paul, using the name 'George(s) Guyou', took refuge in Scotland with his family during the 1890s. Wanted by the French police in connection with the anarchist outrages, with which he had nothing to do, Paul Reclus became one of Geddes's right-hand men at the Outlook Tower, and a lifelong friend, later settling in Montpellier (Fig.40).[14] The two families eventually intermarried. Geddes and Elisée Reclus further had prolonged contact over the project for Reclus's Great Globe, planned for the 1900 Paris Exposition, but never built (Fig.41). They remained in close touch until Reclus's death in 1905.[15]

Augustin Hamon (1862-1945) (Fig.42) was recommended to Geddes by Paul Reclus, probably through the Brussels connection. Another anarchist writer, Hamon had been advised to leave France in summer 1894, and was staying in London. 'Georges Guyou' wrote to Geddes on 2 January 1895, suggesting that Hamon stay in Edinburgh for a month in one of the University Halls. He quickly made friends with John Duncan and the Geddes circle and was very taken with the atmosphere at Riddle's Court. By the time he left he had been engaged to give 10 lectures on '*la France actuelle*' ('Contemporary France') at the Summer Meeting that year. His links with Geddes appear to relate more to artistic matters than to political or social thought. As he put it, 'there is a whole clan of artists around Geddes'.[16]

41. Elisée Reclus, Project for Terrestrial Globe, 1897-8. © National Library of Scotland.

42. Augustin Hamon, 1895, from *Les Hommes d'aujourd'hui*.

This is perhaps the place to say *en passant* that the Geddes circle in Edinburgh was a much more mixed one culturally than that of his French contacts. In France, apart from the anarchist intellectuals, he was mainly in touch with the official academy, men of letters or science, whereas in Edinburgh his circle was of free-thinking progressives, including many artists and especially women – new women, craftswomen, singers. At any rate, Hamon in his letters to Lucien Pissarro refers principally to artistic matters, rather than science or politics. He refers to Geddes as 'my friend and [John] Duncan's, and an art lover, who wishes to turn Edinburgh into an artistic centre'.[17]

The Franco-Scottish Society

We now have to jump to a somewhat different circle, and it is surprising how Geddes managed to reach such eminent people in the French system so quickly. But the enterprise was not his alone. This concerns the setting up of the Franco-Scottish Society in 1895-6. Already in 1890, following the 1889 Exhibition, Geddes had linked up with Lavisse and Pasteur (no less) to form a 'Comité Franco-écossais', mainly relating to student exchanges, with Paul Melon as administrator. But the lift-off for the new Society seems to have come when a Scottish lawyer in Paris, Thomas Barclay (1853-1940) gave it a push a few years later.

Barclay and Geddes were contemporaries and world-class networkers.[18] They held the first meeting of the Scottish branch in Edinburgh in October 1895, presided over by Lord Reay. The official opening was held in the Sorbonne in 1896. Pasteur had just died, in 1895, but the roll-call of members at these first two meetings sounds like a branch meeting of the 'Republique des Professeurs' combined with the 'high heidyins' of (mostly academic) Scottish society. Among the French were a swathe of eminent academics: Octave Gréard, Rector of the University of Paris, the historian Ernest Lavisse, the Hellenist Alfred Croiset; the scientist Emile Duclaux, Pasteur's successor; Emile Boutroux, Charles Gide, Louis Liard, architect of university reform in France – most of whom Geddes had already recruited for one or other of his exchange schemes. Veteran politician Jules Simon presided, and the French president Félix Faure attended the evening event. Alongside them were several members of the aristocracy in both countries. It was on this occasion that a line reproduction of John Duncan's drawing of Joan of Arc and her guard of Scottish archers was presented to the French branch (with an extra artist's proof for President Faure).

Geddes promptly added many more names to his address book.[19] I am not sure how many of these people he knew well before this initiative. Thomas Barclay later claimed the Franco-Scottish Society was a dry run for the *entente cordiale*, a question which we will not seek to resolve here. However there is no doubt that the great and good from both sides were involved in the early manifestations of the Franco-Scottish Society. Its later history, while interesting, had a less high profile than its beginnings. Neither the political clout desired by Barclay, nor the culturally progressive role envisaged by Geddes ever really came about, although it has remained a focus for friendly exchanges between Scotland and France for over a hundred years.[20]

Making the networks work: the Paris Exhibition of 1900

For the 1900 Exposition Universelle in Paris, Geddes orchestrated his most ambitious project yet, the International Assembly or Ecole internationale: in effect a four-language summer school running throughout the exhibition. This represents in a way both the culmination and the apogee of Geddes's cultivation of his French networks. It is worth noting that at this moment in history, relations between France and Britain were not at all cordial. They had almost come to blows in 1898 over the Fashoda incident, the Anglo-French confrontation in the Sudan. The South African War (known as the Boer War in Britain and 'la guerre du Transvaal' in France) had seen jingoism in Britain and strong pro-Boer sentiment in France. The second Dreyfus trial, in 1899, when Captain Dreyfus was once again found guilty by a French military tribunal (before accepting a presidential pardon), had inflamed British opinion against France. British visitors were tempted to boycott the Paris Exhibition (Mafeking was relieved in May 1900) and Geddes initially feared for his project.[21]

A much larger version of the Edinburgh Summer Meetings, financed in part by Sir Robert Pullar of Perth, and drawing on some of the usual lecturers, plus many more, the Ecole Internationale turned out to be quite successful. It consisted of talks on every conceivable subject, visits to pavilions and sites, museums and galleries, industrial locations etc, with the aim of making the exhibition a centre of knowledge. Geddes had enlisted the support of the British Association for the Advancement of Science in autumn 1899, and activated all his French intellectual links. Enthusiasm on both sides of the Channel resulted in an eminent set of patrons: Léon Bourgeois, the former French prime minister and minister of education,was president, with support from a number of professors and educationists, some of them only recently encountered during the Franco-Scottish launch. They included many we have already met: Charles Gide, Emile Duclaux, Lavisse, Gréard, Liard and others. The lecturers were of several nationalities, including American, but with a 'hard core' of regular and devoted Geddes helpers from Edinburgh.

The success of the whole enterprise was summed up by the academic Emile Bourgeois in his report. It operated for four months, employing 100 lecturers, 8 secretaries, and 10 other staff, laying on 300 formal lectures, 800 talks, and 450 guided visits to a total of visitors/students running into tens of thousands: 'Many a university does not offer as much in a semester', as Geddes later said. Geddes was also an active participant at the International Conference on the Social Sciences held during September 1900, organized by Dick May, at which almost all his academic contacts were present (including Seignobos, Gide, etc) – a gathering described by Christophe Prochasson as the 'Republican establishment in session'.[22] That summer was the occasion for Geddes to make further intellectual contacts with French thinkers, notably Emile Durkheim and Henri Bergson, with whom he later corresponded.

While the Summer School was an extraordinary feat of organization but not really controversial, the last of Patrick Geddes's Paris schemes in 1900 was quixotic, ambitious and provocative. Specially-designed and much admired national pavilions, showing cultural displays for each country, had been built along the left bank of the Seine opposite the Grand Palais for the duration of the Exposition Universelle. They were known as the 'Rue des Nations'. Geddes proposed (as the official report explains)[23] to save them in permanent form after the Fair closed in the autumn. He suggested they should become international museums (one for peace, one for the sea,

43. Rue des Nations, Exposition Universelle, 1900, from *The Art Journal*, 1901, p.31. © National Library of Scotland.

one for experimental science, etc). The idea was to de-nationalize them, with their original national identities being absorbed into international and 'peaceful' concepts. Geddes campaigned energetically, and worked his address book during the latter part of 1900 and early 1901. No doubt he started via his original contacts: we know that Lavisse, Gréard, Liard and Duclaux all helped him; Léon Bourgeois threw his not inconsiderable weight into the balance. Eventually, the proposal was supported by a range of diverse personalities, including no fewer than four ministers in the French cabinet, one of whom, significantly, was the future architect of the *entente cordiale*, the French foreign secretary Théophile Delcassé. The scheme eventually foundered, in part on legal and technical grounds – the buildings were only temporary – and partly because the new nationalist majority of the Paris municipal council was against it. (The British Foreign Office was none too keen either.) Another opponent was the notorious Edouard Drumont, an extreme anti-semitic forerunner of Jean-Marie Le Pen, and opponent to anything that smacked of internationalism. Drumont wrote a ferocious article in his newpaper *La Libre Parole*, saying in effect 'I don't presume to tell Professor Geddes how to re-arrange the skyline of Princes Street!'[24]

Defeated by a mixture of bureaucracy and real technical problems, as well as political opposition, the 'Rue des Nations' was one project Geddes had to abandon. Thereafter he turned to pastures new – international ones. After 1900, although his personal friendships with French contacts persisted, his extraordinary career, focussing increasingly on town planning and the environment, took him in ever new and more far-flung directions. Only after his retirement, in 1924, did he really return to France, and then it was to be for his swansong, the creation of the Collège des Ecossais in Montpellier, a city with which he had entertained strong connections from his youth. His scheme for a student residence is described by Helen Meller as 'completely impractical', and so it was in many ways, but it survived its creator, and has inspired the Patrick Geddes Association in France, launched by Professor A. Schimmerling, editor of the periodical, *Le Carré bleu*.[25]

Conclusion

Geddes's final initiative of 1900, the Rue des Nations appeal, may help us to decipher some of the hidden threads behind his networking in Third Republic France. They were more political than might at first appear. Although he was studiously non-affiliated to any political party, he could not help being attached to liberal progressive causes. During the late 1890s, as noted earlier, Britain and France were at odds, each country considering the other to be in the wrong over Fashoda, Dreyfus, South Africa, etc. Geddes's contacts were chiefly among those who took the side of 'justice' and liberalism against the prevailing mode of their own country's official policy. His British contacts (about which space does not permit discussion: they include James Bryce and W.T. Stead), tended to be radical (that is to say non-Unionist and non-colonialist) Liberals, opposed to the Boer War.

Geddes's French contacts tended above all, during the 1890s, to be supporters of the Dreyfus cause, which divided France. Some were very strongly committed, (e.g. Duclaux), and many, such as family friend Marie Bonnet, were in the Ligue des Droits de l'Homme. Ex-premier Léon Bourgeois is a particularly important figure; 'a closet Dreyfusist in 1898', and a freemason, he was the key figure in 'Solidarism', the philosophy of mutual help between the different classes of society, which dominated the1900 social science congress, and was indeed the prevailing philosophy of the moderate French republicans of the time. By contrast, we have already noted that one of the most violent anti-Dreyfus forces, the anti-semitic Edouard Drumont, had taken a dislike to Geddes's schemes.

There was therefore a sort of 'freemasonry' of a less formal kind linking Patrick Geddes's French networks. They almost all took the side of Dreyfus during the Affair (1895-1899). And they cut across the usual hierarchies which marked the French university system for example, so that humble lecturers from the provinces taught alongside eminent professors from the Sorbonne at the Summer Meetings. Geddes, with the particular advantage in France of being a foreigner, was equally at home with the marquesses and earls who joined the Franco-Scottish Society, with the mild-mannered but determined anarchists, or with the working men whom he encouraged to come to his summer school, as well as with a whole procession of French academics and politicians. As his friend Demolins remarked: 'I have rarely met anyone possessing to such a high degree the art of attracting and keeping people he has once conquered'.

Appendix: principal members of Geddes's French networks

[MS = attached to the Musée Social; D= identified as being pro-Dreyfus]

Scientific: H. Lacaze-Duthiers; L. Pasteur; C. Flahault (Montpellier); Y. Delage; later Emile Duclaux (D)

Le Playists: E. Demolins; P. de Rousiers; Abbé Klein; J. Bailhache; L. Poinsard [links to Jules Siegfried (MS)]

Anarchists: P. Kropotkin; Elisée Reclus; Paul Reclus; A. Hamon

Summer Meetings: All those in 2 and 3 above, plus A. Espinas (D) (MS); Paul Desjardins (D); G. Monod (D); H. Trocmé; H. Mazel; L. Marillier (D); Firmin Roz; Delvolvé; Caudel; Mlle Marie Bonnet (D); and others

Franco-Scots: E. Lavisse; Pasteur; Bardoux; Beljame; Bichat; Boutmy (MS); Boutroux; Bréal (D); Brouardel; Bufnoir; Alfred Croiset (D); Duclaux (D); Espinas (D) Comte de Franqueville; Ch. Gide; Himly; Gréard; Liard; Jules Simon; Paul Meyer (D); de Vogué; and others

Paris International Assembly 1900: Patrons/committee (not lecturers): Léon Bourgeois (D); Emile Bourgeois (D); Gréard; Liard; Prince R. Bonaparte; Espinas (D); Lyon-Caen (D) (MS); Malet; Melon; Brouardel; Lavisse; H.Poincaré; J. Clarétie; Mabilleau (MS); Ch. Gide; G. Perrot; J. Siegfried; P. Melon; Mlle Dick May (MS; Conf. Soc. Sci); and others

Rue des Nations Project: Millerand, Delcassé, Cauvin; L. Bourgeois; Liard; Duclaux; Prince R. Bonaparte; Coppée (non-D); E. Bourgeois; L. Herbette; G. Moch; Ch. Normand; J. Labusquière; F. Schrader; and others

Patrick Geddes's Address Book, 1900: Caudel; Siegfried; Seignobos (D); Lavisse; Duclaux; Delage; Desjardins; Schrader; Planes; Le Foyer; Plessat; Metin; Guerard; and others

NOTES

1. Special number of *The Edinburgh Review*, on Patrick Geddes, No.88, 1992, p.3.

2. There are several biographies of Geddes, three by Philip Boardman: *Esquisse de l'oeuvre éducatrice de Patrick Geddes*, Montpellier1936; *Patrick Geddes: Maker of the Future*, Chapel Hill 1944; and *The Worlds of Patrick Geddes: Biologist, Town Planner, Re-educator, Peace-Warrior*, London 1978. The most recent full-length work is the excellent critical biography by Helen Meller, *Patrick Geddes: Social Evolutionist and City Planner*, London 1990 (paperback 1993), which gives a bibliography and lists primary sources. The Geddes papers are in several locations. Two of the largest deposits are in the University of Strathclyde (hereafter PGA/US); and the National Library of Scotland (NLS) in Edinburgh. As his wife Anna Geddes remarked, 'All Pat's enterprises are linked', copy of letter dated 5 August 1900, NLS Ms 10577.

3. *Student Days in France*, Outlook Tower booklet, quoted Boardman, *Esquisse*, pp. 91-2.

4. *Paris University*, Outlook Tower booklet, quoted by Meller, p.34. Patrick Geddes and V.V. Branford, *Our Social Inheritance*, London 1919, pp.344-5.

5. Quoted in Boardman, *Esquisse*, p.15.

6. Meller, p.126.

7. On 1890, see Anna Geddes, 'Montpellier and its ancient university' in *The (Scottish) Art Review*, Vol.3, 1890, pp.130-4. We know from Flahault's correspondence with Geddes (PGA/US, T.GED 12/3/2 letters written in May and June 1890) that Anna's article was translated into French by 'Monsieur Valéry', who was a law student at Montpellier at the time (probably the brother of Paul Valéry the poet). See these and further letters in NLS Ms 10525 for first references to Charles Gide (uncle of André) and Ernest Lavisse.

8. See Meller, p. 43 for further details.

9. On the Summer Meetings see Meller, pp.92 ff. There are many papers concerning them in PGA/US and NLS. Demolins published his first impressions in several numbers of his newsletter, *Le Mouvement Social* (supplement to *La Science Sociale*) in 1892-3 (pp.77-86, 97-106, 126-33). See also B. Kalaora and A. Savoye, *Les inventeurs oubliés: Le Play et ses continuateurs*, Seyssel 1989, esp. pp.150-9; and *Les Etudes Sociales*, Nos 127-8, 1998 (all available in Musée Social, Paris).

10. See *Le Musée Social en son temps (collectif)*, Paris 1998, esp. pp.43ff. on Dick May, and J. Horne, *A Social Laboratory for Modern France: the Musée Social and the Origins of the Welfare State*, Durham N.C 2002. 'Dick May' was a pseudonym.

11. *Revue Internationale de l'Enseignement*, 15 May 1896 (copy in PGA/US).

12. Boardman, *Worlds of Patrick Geddes*, pp.87, 105. On links with Kropotkin, see Macdonald, pp.87-8 below, and Mavor, *Windows on the Street of the World*, Vol.2, pp.91-2, 119-20.

13. Elisée Reclus, *Correspondance*, Paris 1925, Vol.3, pp.188-9. For overviews of Reclus's life, see M. Fleming, *The Anarchist Way to Socialism: Élisée Reclus*, London 1979; Béatrice Griblin, 'Élisée Reclus' in *Geographers: Biobibliography*, Vol.3, London 1979. The Geddes archives contain many letters to and from the entire Reclus family.

14. On Paul Reclus see the article in J. Maitron et al., *Dictionnaire biographique du mouvement ouvrier français*, Paris various dates, under his name. See also Meller, pp.15-16.

15. On the Great Globe, see S. Reynolds, 'After Dreyfus and before the entente:

Patrick Geddes's cultural diplomacy at the Paris Exhibition of 1900', in M. Cornick and C. Crossley, eds, *Problems in French History*, Basingstoke 2000, and references in the Reclus papers, Biblothèque Nationale, Paris, Département des Manuscrits, NAF, 22916, and NLS MS 10625, f.229.

16. See Thomson, pp.47, 61 above. On Hamon's introduction to Geddes, see the correspondence with Georges Guyou in NLS Ms 10564 for January 1895 and n.17 below. Hamon was a radical thinker hard to pigeonhole. With his wife Henriette, he translated all Shaw's plays into French. For details see P. Gaillou, doctoral thesis, *G.B. Shaw et Augustin Hamon: les premiers temps d'une correspondance*, Université de Bretagne Occidentale, Brest, 1998, and the same author's 'Une itinéraire politique, Augustin Hamon', *Kreuz*, No.10, 1999, pp. 200-27. See also the article on him in Maitron (n. 14), under his name.

17. Pissarro archives, Ashmolean Museum, Oxford, letters of 22 January and 3 February 1895.

18. See their correspondence in PGA/US, T.GED 12/1/15 and NLS Ms 10527, 27 March 1895, about whom to contact.

19. See his 'address book', list of Paris addresses in 1900 (PGA/US, T.GED 6/1/5).

20. On the early history of the Franco-Scottish Society, see *Transactions of the Franco-Scottish Society*, 1897; T. Barclay, *Thirty Years: Anglo-French Reminiscences 1876-1906*, London 1914, chs 11, 13; and *The Franco-Scottish Society Bulletin*, No.24, May 1995 (Centenary Year), especially the article by A. Steele. The Society's archives are deposited in the National Library of Scotland.

21. For full references to this section, which is largely based on papers in PGA/US, see Reynolds (n.15), and Meller, pp.113-17.

22. C. Prochasson, *Les années électriques*, Paris 1991, pp. 230-1.

23. Alfred Picard, *Rapport général: le bilan d'un siècle 1801-1900*, 6 vols, Paris 1906-7, Vol.6, p.288.

24. Cutting in PGA/US, T.GED 6/3/5.

25. Meller, pp. 315-17.

V. Patrick Geddes's Generalism: from Edinburgh's Old Town to Paris's Universal Exhibition

MURDO MACDONALD

Patrick Geddes's thinking was part of a tradition of intellectual generalism in Scotland, a tradition within which both interdisciplinarity and visual methods were highly valued. The classic account is *The Democratic Intellect* by George Davie. An understanding of Geddes and his cultural revival milieu must take note of this tradition, both for its visual and its interdisciplinary aspects. What flows from this is an appreciation that Geddes's role as an advocate of visual art and, indeed, of the visual in general, is central to his wider achievement.

In the closing years of the 19th century, the Edinburgh educationist, Simon Somerville Laurie, singled out Patrick Geddes 'as the Scot who had best kept up the French connection' in matters academic and cultural.[1] France was a point of reference and inspiration for Geddes throughout his career from his student days in Brittany and Paris in the 1870s to his establishment of a Scots College at Montpellier in the 1920s;[2] indeed he died at Montpellier in 1932.

A notable example of Geddes's French connection was his encouragement, in the mid-1890s, of substantial French, Belgian and Breton contributions to his magazine *The Evergreen*. *The Evergreen* included images strongly influenced by developments in French art on the cusp of Symbolism and Post-Impressionism. It is worth detailing these *Evergreen* contributions in full. In order of publication, the very first of them is an image by Paul Sérusier, *Pastorale bretonne* (Fig.44), which appears in 1895 in *The Book of Spring*, the first issue of *The Evergreen*. It is immediately followed by a piece by Dorothy Herbertson entitled 'Spring in Languedoc' and a little later one finds a piece in French on 'La littérature

44. Paul Sérusier, *Pastorale bretonne* from *The Evergreen, The Book of Spring*, 1895, p.77.

LA CITÉ DU BON ACCORD[1]

LA Joie par excellence est de trouver un ami et de lui montrer qu'on l'aime. Oui, la Joie par excellence, car l'Amour même, avec tous ses emportements, n'a sa vraie grandeur, n'est durable que par la fervente amitié.

Mais en dehors de ce haut sentiment qui dépasse de beaucoup la simple fraternité, puisqu'elle suppose une association complète des volontés et des actes, combien d'impulsions naturelles auxquelles on donne ordinairement le nom d'"amitiés", et qui, sans mériter cette appellation glorieuse, n'en sont pas moins des sentiments très nobles et qu'il faudrait pleinement satisfaire! La sympathie voudrait souvent s'élancer de l'homme à l'homme, mais pour mille causes étrangères elle ne se manifeste point. Que de fois chacun de nous a-t-il ainsi rencontré des personnes que d'un coup d'œil il a reconnues comme des amis en puissance, comme des êtres avec lesquels il voudrait échanger des pensées sincères, mais qui pour lui ne seront jamais que des ombres, destinées bientôt à fuir de sa mémoire : ce ne sont guère que des apparences vaines malgré

[1] This article is placed in the section 'Autumn in the North' since it has been suggested by a recent visit from its writer. The foremost geographer in Europe, M. Reclus, is also the joint-apostle with Tolstoi of the higher Anarchism. Both characteristics of his thought are thus represented in his title; his generous hopefulness most of all.

45. (*Above*) Headpiece and opening paragraph of 'La Cité du bon accord' by Elisée Reclus from *The Evergreen, The Book of Autumn*, 1895, p.103. © National Library of Scotland.

46. E.A. Hornel, *Madame Chrysanthème* from *The Evergreen, The Book of Autumn*, 1895, p.101. © National Library of Scotland.

nouvelle en France' by Charles Sarolea of Edinburgh University. Along with those overtly French or French-orientated contributions is the strong influence of Sérusier, and indeed others of the Pont-Aven school, on the work of the Scottish artist Charles Mackie, who contributes two illustrations, along with the cover and title-page designs. It was Mackie's contact with Sérusier that led to the latter contributing *Pastorale bretonne* to the first issue of *The Evergreen* and on the basis of correspondence between the two artists, Clare Willsdon has raised the intriguing possibility that Sérusier actually painted a mural for Geddes's flat in Ramsay Garden.[3]

In the second volume of *The Evergreen*, published later the same year, the broadly French aspect is equally strong. There one finds William Sharp's translation of *Les Flaireurs* by the Belgian writer Charles van Lerberghe.[4] A few pages later is a piece by Abbé Félix Klein published in its original French. This paper, 'Le dilettantisme', characterises the literary movement of Renan, Jules Lemaitre, Anatole France and Maurice Barrès, as superficial. It is immediately followed by Edith Wingate Rinder's English version of the Breton legend Amel and Penhor.[5] Here also is another piece in French, 'La cité du bon accord' (Fig.45), by Geddes's friend the anarchist geographer Elisée Reclus, who is described in a footnote as 'the joint-apostle with Tolstoi of the higher Anarchism'. And again Mackie's illustrations show their Pont-Aven influence. Another image, by the Glasgow painter E.A. Hornel, takes as its subject a Japanese woman, but the title is *Madame Chrysanthème*, a reference to the story by Pierre Loti (Fig.46).

The next *Evergreen* volume, *The Book of Summer*, published in 1896, contains

47. John Duncan, *The Way to Rheims* from *The Evergreen, The Book of Summer*, 1896, p.99. © National Library of Scotland.

another version of a Breton legend, 'Telen Rumengol', by Edith Wingate Rinder, and another piece in French, 'Vers l'unité', a meditation on the common aspects of the major global religions, by Abbé Félix Klein. Along with Mackie's images is one by Robert Brough,[6] another Scottish artist with close links to France and, indeed, to Brittany, and two by Andrew K. Womrath, which are given French titles. Here also one finds John Duncan's Joan of Arc illustration, *The Way to Rheims* (Fig.47) of which more below. *The Book of Winter*, the final volume of *The Evergreen*, contains Paul Desjardins's 'Il neige'; a further Breton legend by Rinder, 'Saint Efflamm and King Arthur'; a piece by Elisée Reclus's brother, Elie Reclus, entitled 'Pourquoi des guirlandes vertes à Noel', and 'A devolution of terror' by Catherine A. Janvier. Also here is a piece on Breton custom by M. Clothilde Balfour, 'The Black Month'.

Thus although *The Evergreen* is correctly described as a product of the Scottish Celtic revival, it is a Celtic revival product which has at its heart a strand of Francophone culture and commentary. And again, in the final volume as in all the others, there are illustrations by Charles Mackie. Mackie is a most interesting figure not least because of his close links with Gauguin and Sérusier. The influence of Pont-Aven inspired synthetism is clear in his work. One can thus consider the Breton primitivism of the Pont-Aven school as an aspect of the pan-Celticism of the late 19th century.[7] More widely, Willsdon has noted the affinities of both Mackie and John Duncan 'with

Continental Symbolism's ideology of mural painting as an affective medium affording entry into dreams and emotional states', and she goes on to note Duncan's reading of Sâr Péladan's, as well as Burne-Jones's theories.[8] In an *Evergreen*-related mural completed in the mid-1890s, Duncan and Geddes had drawn attention to the links between France and Scotland from the perspective of history. Duncan's painting of *Joan of Arc and her Scots Guard* (Fig.13)[9] was originally located in the common room of the University Hall residence of St Giles House, a few hundred yards east of Ramsay Lodge. This work was first mooted by Geddes in a letter to Duncan sent in November 1895 in which he notes a suggestion from Andrew Lang[10] 'of the Franco-Scottish society' for a painting of Joan of Arc with her bodyguard of Scottish Archers.[11] In due course a black-and-white version of the design appeared in *The Evergreen: The Book of Summer* in 1896 under the title *The Way to Rheims* (Fig.47). It has the caption 'Franco-Scottish Society – Sorbonne, 18th April 1896', the date which marked the official opening of the new society in Paris.[12] Consideration of Andrew Lang can extend perception of this Francophile milieu a little further for in 1896 Lang was bringing to fruition another project related to Joan of Arc, the publication of his novel *A Monk of Fife*. This tells the tale of a Scottish cleric from St Andrews in the France of Saint Joan and it was illustrated throughout by the Arts and Crafts designer Selwyn Image.[13]

It is thus in the context of Geddes's established interest in France that in 1900 the linking point of the diverse strands of his internationalism shifted from Edinburgh to Paris. The annual Edinburgh Summer Meeting was transformed into the Paris International Assembly, an educational complement to the Exposition Universelle. Geddes had a great regard for the social value of major international exhibitions. For him an intelligently structured spectacle was the starting point for creative thought. In 1887 he had published an extended critique entitled *Industrial Exhibitions and Modern Progress* in which he exhorted the organisers of future industrial exhibitions to 'take real and detailed heed of the claims of Art, Science, and Political Economy'. The Exposition Universelle in Paris in 1900 seems to have met Geddes's prescription to a significant degree. Geddes's old friend James Mavor was in Paris at the time and he comments that the exhibition 'illustrated Geddes's theme more fully' than any other yet held, quite apart from Geddes's own contribution.[14] Geddes's Paris International Assembly was an ambitious undertaking. Its extensive lecture programme began in mid May and continued to the end of October and lecturers included Outlook Tower regulars such as Geddes himself, Thomas Marr, and John Duncan.[15] In addition there were a number of American speakers. This transatlantic involvement reflected a new dimension of Geddes's internationalism, which he had begun to develop in earnest as part of his efforts to gather support, both financial and intellectual, for the International Association, a body which Geddes had created to support the Paris International Assembly.[16] Geddes's American contacts included the psychologists Stanley Hall and William James and the educator John Dewey. Another was the social reformer and educator Jane Addams who had the previous year established Hull House in Chicago along lines suggested by Toynbee Hall in London, a development that had also influenced Geddes. Addams lectured for Geddes in Paris, and the Chicago link was underlined by the appointment of Geddes's close collaborator, John Duncan, as professor of art at the newly formed Chicago Institute, where he worked until 1903.[17]

James Mavor provides further insight into the wider intellectual milieu of which Geddes was part in Paris in 1900. Mavor himself made a number of visits to Rodin in his studio and recalls meeting the anarchist Elisée Reclus by chance at a lecture on Rodin given by the art critic Camille Mauclair.[18] Reclus was not only a friend of Geddes and an *Evergreen* contributor, as already noted, but he had taught at Geddes's Summer Meetings in Edinburgh, and had also published, in 1895, a notable essay 'The evolution of cities', which not only prefigures in its title Geddes's later book, *Cities in Evolution*, but contains an account of the Geddes-motivated work in urban conservation undertaken by the Edinburgh Social Union in the 1880s. Reclus writes:

> We are told that in Edinburgh, the lovely Scottish capital, pious hands are at work ... breaking in upon its picturesque but unclean wynds, and transforming them gradually, house by house – leaving every inhabitant at home as before, but in a cleaner and more beautiful home, where the air and light come through; grouping friends with friends, and giving them places of reunion for social intercourse and the enjoyment of art. Little by little a whole street, retaining its original character, only without the dirt and the smells, comes out fresh and crisp, like the flower springing clean beneath the foot without a single sod being stirred around the mother plant.[19]

Mavor's further reminiscences of Geddes's milieu in Paris are intriguing. Not least of these, again linking Geddes with an anarchist thinker, is an account of an excursion around the city on which Mavor accompanied the assembled Geddes and Kropotkin families. Kropotkin had met both Geddes and Mavor when visiting Edinburgh in 1886, indeed the Russian's biographers describe Mavor and Geddes as among his closest scientific friends.[20] Earlier in his invaluable autobiography, Mavor gives an account of the formation of this network of cultural, political and scientific figures in the Edinburgh of the 1880s. He recalls meeting Kropotkin for the first time one evening at a party at Geddes's flat.[21] Among those attending was Thomas Kirkup, author of the article on socialism for the ninth edition of the *Encylopaedia Britannica*.[22] Mavor comments that 'Kropotkin and I alternately hammered Marx and Kirkup spoke up for him, and we had an excellent discussion.'[23] It is in the context of such gatherings that Geddes's thinking as expressed in his pamphlet *Co-operation Versus Socialism* (published in 1888) must be seen. There Geddes acknowledges both Kirkup and Kropotkin, and he writes that 'few people adequately realise how good a case can ... be stated for socialism; still fewer know how an even better case can be stated for anarchism; while fewest of all yet recognise in those apparently strange developments of modern thought much of the oldest, commonest, and most enduring wisdom of the human race.'[24]

This, then, is the background for Mavor joining the Geddes and Kropotkin families for their tour of Paris in 1900. Their guide was the elderly Parisian communist Le Français who had been behind the barricades as a boy in 1830, and again in 1848 and 1871. Mavor notes that Le Français showed them 'how certain parts of Paris were readily convertible into miniature fortresses'. This has more than just an obvious historical interest for such information gives real insight into the origins and development of the city, the nature of its communities and how they are physically defined, topics of central interest to Geddes as a pioneer of the developing discipline of town planning. Geddes and Mavor took such considerations further in a walking tour in northern France in the late summer of 1900, reflecting on the *ronds-points* of the forest of St Cloud, which afforded rendezvous for hunters, as the putative origin of the plan of the city of Paris.[25]

Mavor makes clear Geddes's wider international links in his reference to the presence in Geddes's circle in Paris of Swami Vivekananda and his disciple, the Irishwoman Margaret Noble, better known as Sister Nivedita. Mavor's account is not wholly accurate, for he assumes that Vivekananda and Nivedita first met that year in Paris, whereas it seems they had met some five years earlier,[26] but the important point here is that they were closely connected with Geddes in Paris. Seven years earlier at the World Parliament of Religions in Chicago[27] Vivekananda had 'presented Hinduism to the world at large as a major religion, emphasising its antiquity.'[28] Taking his lead from the ideas of Ramakrishna, Vivekananda articulated the case for Hindu revival. In Paris he lectured on Indian art, rejecting theories of Hellenistic influence and underlining the independent value of the early Buddhist art of India.[29]

In due course Nivedita was to develop this position as was, in a more systematic way, another of Geddes's friends, Ananda Coomaraswamy. Vivekananda died in 1902, but Nivedita continued to be one of Geddes's valued intellectual allies up until her death in 1911. Also present in Paris was the eminent Indian scientist Jagadis Chandra Bose. Sister Nivedita numbered his wife among her closest friends, and 20 years later Patrick Geddes – who by then was making a major contribution to town planning and educational developments in India – was to be his biographer.[30] In a memoir of Nivedita printed in *The Sociological Review* in 1913, Geddes recalled their first meeting[31] and how it 'continued into intimacy and collaboration during the following summer, at the meeting of the International Association which became the Summer School of the Paris Exhibition of that in many ways memorable year.'[32] Nivedita had much in common with Geddes. Both complemented their dedication to cultural

revival with a passionate interest in new educational methods: indeed prior
to her involvement with Vivekananda, Margaret Noble had been a respected
advocate of the methods of Pestallozzi and Froebel.[33] In addition, one should
note that in the context of this essay Geddes's interest in educational ideas
can be set firmly in an Auld Alliance context. His generalism has firm roots
in the Scottish tradition, but it gains from the generalist thinking of Auguste
Comte (1798-1857) and, in particular, of Frédéric Le Play (1806-1882),
and his follower Edmond Demolins.

   Developing this point from the perspective of Scottish influence, Geddes's
work is part of what George Davie has called the 'democratic intellect',
that is to say the type of philosophically-considered interdisciplinary thinking
characteristic of Scotland in the 18th and 19th centuries.[34] Davie's discussion provides the context for Geddes's generalism and any consideration of
Geddes's engagement with the thinking of other generalist figures such as
Ruskin, Comte, Le Play and Spencer, must be seen as driven from this
Scottish intellectual source. From the perspective of the French educational tradition, although Geddes's interest in Comte is often taken for
granted, he himself in *The Evergreen* is at pains to make clear his view of
Comte's limitations, and his preference for the thinking of Le Play:

> Auguste Comte is popularly supposed to be a radical, a democratic man of mod-
> ern science. But he makes his contributions to sociology from the standpoint of
> hierarchy of feeling and genius, of the aristocracy of action and thought. Con-
> versely, it is Frederic Le Play ... who is popularly supposed even in his own
> country to make his appeal to capitalist and conservative, to aristocrat and
> priest, who has really established for us the vital doctrine of all democracy ...

Geddes continues in a direct critique of Comte by pointing out that
although he sees the great stream of Humanity he 'calls attention mainly
to the Calendar of Great Men, to the men of genius as Her chief servants –
for him, proletarian and woman are little better than grown children, to be
guided and governed for ever by patrician and priest.' In contrast Geddes
the egalitarian evolutionist argues in favour of Le Play, arguing that for him
'worker and woman unite to form the elementary human family, and from
them, not only by bodily descent, but social descent, from their everyday
life and labour, there develops the whole fabric of institutions and ideas,
temporal and spiritual.'[35] Geddes does not reject the concept of a 'Calendar
of Great Men', indeed it is the frame of reference for his later *Masques of
Learning*. However, he is at pains to argue that what we call people of genius are emergent properties of a wider, evolving system. And this system
exists as an integrated social fabric, not as a system in which one discrete
group has the quasi-divine function of guiding another.

   This critique of Comte predates Geddes's involvement with the Paris
exhibition of 1900. Geddes's continuing inspiration from France after that
date is reflected in a work published more than a decade later. This is the
text of his remarkable historical masques, eventually collected under the

title of *Dramatisations of History*.[36] In one passage he pointedly incorpo-
rates the history of the Scots College in Paris, whose revival he had
promoted since 1890. The idea eventually became reality in Geddes's Scots
College at Montpellier, which was still in the process of development at the
time of his death. For example, in a scene performed in Edinburgh in 1911
and in London in 1912, Geddes, writing of the time of Robert Bruce, when
Scotland was to be found re-establishing itself in the wake of successful
resistance to English invasion, notes that:

> the independence of Scotland had to be maintained – and this intellectually and
> spiritually, as well as by the material forces of the Franco-Scottish Alliance which
> was thus necessitated. Hence Bruce founded, or rather renewed, for the Scots at
> Paris the famous College des Ecossais. This, as rebuilt from its medieval ruin by
> the Bishop of Moray in the sixteenth century, is preserved in good repair by the
> French Commission of National Monuments.

It is clear that Geddes is interested here in educational policy-making as
much as in historical reflection for he continues:

> It well rewards a visit, and not merely on these historic grounds, or for later
> Jacobite associations; but also because its recovery by the Scottish Universities
> can and should now be arranged for, and this in ways helpful to each and every
> interest concerned. Oxford will retain its manifold advantages and charms; but
> our renewal of contacts with the continent generally, with France and with
> Paris, in our day, as of old, the intensest and on the whole, the most educative of
> Universities and cities remains none the less the paramount desideratum of our
> Scottish Universities.

He brings the argument up to date by invoking the importance of France
for major 19th-century scientific pioneers active in Scotland:

> Nor is this less obvious in recent than in ancient times. Loyal to Glasgow and to
> Cambridge as he was, Kelvin was wont to tell how he was aroused to his life-
> work during his wander-year in Paris. In the same way we have heard Lister
> speak, and with even more obvious indebtedness, of his 'honoured master, Louis
> Pasteur.' Nor do our Scottish painters forget their debt to Barbizon. Analogous
> impulses are still available, as every wandering student knows.[37]

He goes on to note that the beginnings of a new collegiate residence in
Paris were linked to developments in Edinburgh in the late 1880s (i.e.
Geddes's University Hall) and refers to negotiations with the French gov-
ernment for the return of the Scots College to the Scottish universities.
Earlier in the same masque Geddes had dramatised the 13th-century growth
of the University of Paris in an imaginary debate between the Dominican
Thomas Aquinas and the Franciscan Duns Scotus, bringing into the pic-
ture not only Dante, as a student, but precursors of Aquinas and Duns
Scotus such as Alcuin and Michael Scot.[38] There he underlined the Franco-
Scottish connection by noting that 'no less than seventeen of the Rectors

of the University of Paris in these early centuries were Scots'. He continues
by making the whole argument current again, emphasising that these historical notes should guide contemporary policy:

> As its students came from far and near, so its teachers wandered, finding wel-
> come and audience in the schools of the towns they settled in. Such 'university
> extension centres,' as we should now call them, became the natural germ of
> new permanent universities, as at Orleans, Oxford, and so on; just as again in
> our time has happened at Dundee,[39] and in various English cities.[40]

By way of conclusion, I note that there is much to be gained from further
reflection on the relationship between Celticism and modernism in a Franco-
Scottish context, and with reference to what one might call the evolutionary historicism of Geddes and his colleagues. For example, John Duncan
visited a key figure of Scottish modernism, J.D. Fergusson, in Paris in 1910,
and Fergusson was later to emphasise that his modernist colourism had a
Celtic dimension.[41] Underlining this Celticism in Fergusson's circle is the
fact that Margaret Morris, who became Fergusson's lifelong partner, danced
at Glastonbury in 1913, the same year she met him in Paris.[42] Morris was
a pioneer of modern dance and Glastonbury was beginning to emerge as
the centre of the English Celtic revival. Those developments at Glastonbury were influenced by both John Duncan and William Sharp.[43] Geddes
and Margaret Morris were also linked, indeed Morris is listed in 1931 in

47. The garden of the Collège des Ecossais, Montpellier. Geddes's friends posing
as Greek goddesses, c.1928. Photo © National Library of Scotland.

the programme for Geddes's Scots College at Montpellier. Her role is as art director of a school to be held at Chateau D'Assas, a building acquired by Geddes to complement the developments at Montpellier. [44]

France was thus as a key intellectual reference point for Patrick Geddes and his colleagues. In 1900 Paris became a wonderful complement to Edinburgh. But Geddes's commitment to France and to French thinking and culture began long before that date and was to continue until his death.

NOTES

1. George E. Davie, writing in *The Democratic Intellect*, Edinburgh 1961, comments that Laurie incarnated 'the spirit of moderation, and from him a network of Scottish influences would seem to have radiated in all directions'. He goes on to note that Laurie, in encouraging his student, Stewart Robertson, to study in Paris, suggested he contact Geddes, and this is the context for the quotation from Laurie. The source of Davie's comment is Stewart Robertson's invaluable account of Geddes, *A Moray Loon.*

2. For a contemporary account see R.C. Buist 'The newest Scots College. Some account of the work of Patrick Geddes', *Scots Magazine*, New Series, Vol.8, No.5, Feb. 1928, pp.321-4.

3. For more on this see Thomson, pp.52-60 above. Willsdon's speculation can be found in 'Paul Serusier the Celt', *Burlington Magazine*, 1984, pp.88-91, and again in Willsdon, *Mural Painting*, p.326.

4. Translated as *The Night-Comers*. Sharp also includes an extensive note on Lerberghe, noting him as the predecessor of Maeterlinck.

5. I am not clear whether Rinder was translating from Breton or French.

6. See also Fowle, p.33 above.

7. Cf. J.G. Fletcher's emphasis on Brittany as part of the Celtic fringe of Europe in his biography of Gauguin. *Paul Gauguin: His Life and Art*, New York 1921, p.55. For an in-depth discussion of Mackie's Pont-Aven links, see Thomson, pp.52-5 above.

8. Willsdon, *Mural Painting*, pp.326-7. Duncan's stylistic debt to Puvis de Chavannes is also clear. It is given context by the publication by Patrick Geddes & Colleagues, in about 1896, of versions of four decorative panels from Puvis's frescoes of St Geneviève in the Pantheon at Paris. These are (perhaps erroneously) advertised as 'lithographed on paper by M. Puvis de Chavannes himself'. These lithographs, under the title *St Geneviève of Paris* are advertised as part of Geddes's Ethic Art Series, on the back cover of *The Evergreen Anthology*, Edinburgh c. 1897. The reference to these prints forms part of a general advertisement for the publications of Patrick Geddes & Colleagues, which includes also publicity for *The Evergreen* and the *Celtic Library* including Edith Wingate Rinder's retellings of Breton legends under the overall title *The Shadow of Arvor*. For more on the Duncan–Puvis de Chavannes link, and the wider context of all this *Evergreen* art, see Fowle, pp.34-7 and 40-3 above.

9. City Art Centre, Edinburgh.

10. Lang is another of the great generalist thinkers of this period, particularly with respect to the development of anthropology and the understanding of myth.

Among much else he was a gatherer of fairy tales and legends (often collaborating with John Duncan's friend William Craigie), and co-translator of what were for many years the standard translations of Homer.

11. Patrick Geddes to John Duncan, 18 Nov. 1895: 'what do you say to a picture suggested by Andrew Lang of the Franco-Scottish Society, of Joan of Arc with her body guard of Scottish Archers?' NLS MS 10508A, f.135.

12. For more on this see Reynolds, p.76 above.

13. The same designer had contributed a title page decoration to the *Scottish Art Review*, a short-lived but fascinating journal published from 1888-90, of which Geddes's close friend James Mavor had been the editor. Mavor, like Lang, is a notable generalist. He was professor of economics at the University of Glasgow and went on to occupy a similar post at the University of Toronto.

14. James Mavor, *My Window on the Street of the World* , Vol. 2, p.107.

15. See also Reynolds, p.77 above.

16. Mavor points out that its full title was 'International Association for the Advancement of Science, Arts and Education – First Assembly at the Paris Exposition of 1900', Mavor, Vol.2, p.107. In 1899 Geddes had persuaded a wealthy Perth businessman, Sir Samuel Pullar, to donate funds to make this International Association possible.

17. Before leaving Chicago Duncan was closely involved in Addams's Hull House, painting a mural panel of Tolstoy towards the end of his stay. My thanks to Frankie Jenkins for giving me access to her research on this point.

18. Mavor, Vol.2, p.111.

19. Elisée Reclus, 'The evolution of cities' in *The Contemporary Review*, 1895, p.67. Reprinted by Jura Books, Petersham New South Wales, in 1995: this quote is from p.20 of the reprint.

20. Kropotkin's other Scottish friends included Keir Hardy, J.S. Keltie, assistant editor of *Nature* and later secretary of the Royal Geographical Society, and William Robertson Smith, who floated the idea that Kropotkin should be appointed to the chair of geography at Cambridge (see George Woodcock and Ivan Avakumovic, *The Anarchist Prince: A Biographical Study of Peter Kropotkin*, London 1950, pp.226-9). Mavor – who shared a Free Kirk background with Robertson Smith (and with Geddes) – sheds light on this relationship: 'It was a matter of deep regret to me that I did not see Robertson Smith in later years ... I used to hear of him, however, from mutual friends. He was on very intimate terms with Prince Kropotkin, and different in many ways as were the two men, there sprang up a deep mutual regard. Robertson Smith was anxious to secure Kropotkin for Cambridge as Professor of Geography. Kropotkin told me that he did not care to compromise his freedom by accepting such a position; but that he felt very pleased that Robertson Smith's friendship had prompted him to so generous a project.' Mavor, Vol.1, p.75.

21. Kropotkin was staying not with the Geddeses but with the classicist and advocate of Celtic revival, John Stuart Blackie. Reflections on Blackie's funeral became the starting point for Geddes's seminal *Evergreen* essay, 'The Scots Renascence'.

22. Published in 1887.

23. Mavor, Vol.2, pp.91-2.

24. Patrick Geddes, *Co-operation Versus Socialism*, Manchester, Co-operative Printing Society 1888, p.20.

25. Mavor, Vol.2, pp.119-20.

26. See Anon, 'Sister Nivedita' in *Eminent Orientalists: Indian, European, American* Madras n.d., pp.257-82.

27. Note that Abbé Klein had referred to this event in his second *Evergreen* piece, 'Vers l'Unité'.

28. J.L. Brockington, *The Sacred Thread: A Short History of Hinduism*, 2nd edn, New Dehli, Oxford University Press 1997, p.182.

29. Tapati Guha-Thakurta, *The Making of a New 'Indian' Art: Artists, Aesthetics and Nationalism in Bengal, c. 1850-1920*, Cambridge 1992, p.173.

30. Patrick Geddes,*An Indian Pioneer of Science: The Life and Work of Sir Jagadis C. Bose*, London 1920.

31. This took place in New York early in 1900.

32. Part of a two-paper feature on Nivedita who is described as 'a late valued member of the Sociological Society' in *The Sociological Review* , Vol.13, pp.242-56. It was reprinted in a pamphlet edited by S.K. Radcliffe, in 1913 entitled *Margaret Noble (Sister Nivedita)*, published by Sherratt & Hughes. A copy can be found in the Strathclyde Geddes archive, T.GED 3/3/35.

33. Anon (n. 26).

34. Davie (n.1). For the wider context of Davie's work see L. Paterson, *Scottish Education in the Twentieth Century*, Edinburgh 2003.

35. 'Flower of the Grass', from *The Evergreen: Book of Summer*, p.58. Geddes gives a more positive appreciation of Comte in his introduction to Susan Liveing's biography of her uncle, John Henry Bridges, *A Nineteenth-Century Teacher: John Henry Bridges*, London 1926.

36. Geddes, *Dramatisations of History*, London 1923. An initial version was published in 1912 as *The Masque of Learning and its Many Meanings, a Pageant of Education through the Ages: Devised and Interpreted by Patrick Geddes*. Then the two volumes later collected as *Dramatisations of History* were published in 1913 in Edinburgh by Patrick Geddes & Colleagues as *The Masque of Ancient Learning* and *The Masque of Medieval and Modern Learning*.

37. *Dramatisations of History*, p.120.

38. Michael Scot had been the subject of one of John Duncan's murals for Ramsay Lodge in the 1890s: see Fig.8 above.

39. Geddes was professor of botany at University College, Dundee, from 1888 to 1919.

40. *Dramatisations of History*, p.117.

41. See e.g. J.D. Fergusson, *Modern Scottish Painting*, Glasgow 1943, pp.84-8.

42. P. Benham, *The Avalonians*, Glastonbury 1993, p.176. See also, for a wider consideration of the influence on dance on Scottish artists in Paris, E. Cumming, S. McGregor & J. Drummond,*Colour Rhythm and Dance: Paintings and Drawings by J. D. Fergusson and his Circle in Paris*, Edinburgh 1985.

43. See Benham (n.42) for numerous references to Sharp and several to Duncan, in the context of Glastonbury.

44. My thanks to Kenny Munro who drew my attention to this via the reference to Morris on p.7 of the prospectus for the Scots College for the session of 1931-2. For a photographic account of Morris's dance of this period see M. Morris & F. Daniels, *Margaret Morris Dancing*, London n.d., c.1930. Morris's system has attracted reference more recently in E.R. Tufte, *Envisioning Information*, Cheshire, Conn. 1990.

Abstracts in English and French

I. Patrick Geddes: Cultivating the Garden of Life

ELIZABETH CUMMING

Patrick Geddes was a complex, creative thinker and scientist. He was concerned with the nature of variation, developing, merging and applying theory from the fields of botany and sociology to urban and cultural renewal. He was absorbed with issues of modernity, renewing links between individuality and collectivism first formulated by the Enlightenment. Through spearheading a range of publications, conferences and programmes, his ideas and work embraced the local, the national and the international. He energised artists and academics equally into progressing standards of physical and spiritual life. Society was an organic whole which evolved through what he called a 'law of progress'. His practice brought together recent and new British and French theory, reflecting particular interests in Ruskin, Comte, Le Play and Taine, and his 1890s urban activities in Edinburgh expressed dynamics of time and place also found in Bergson and Durkheim.

Geddes often spoke of the need for collective cultural memory and understanding. With local artists and architects, he re-energised the core of Edinburgh's physical and intellectual geography at Ramsay Garden, a complex of new and 18th-century buildings. His Summer Meetings of Science and Art attracted some of the most creative minds in France and Scotland, as did the publications of Patrick Geddes & Colleagues, notably *The Evergreen* (1895-6). The Meetings he organised in Paris throughout the 1900 Exposition Universelle followed these quite naturally. France also provided both institutional and personal bedrock to his work, from the foundation of the Franco-Scottish Society in the 1890s to his establishment of the Collège des Ecossais in Montpellier on his retirement there aged seventy.

Patrick Geddes: cultiver le jardin de la vie

Patrick Geddes fut un penseur et un scientifique, complexe et créateur. Il s'occupait de la nature de la variation, développant, unissant, et adaptant au renouvellement urbain et culturel, des théories puisées dans les domaines de la botanique ou de la sociologie. Préoccupé par des questions de modernité, il renoua les liens entre l'individualisme et le collectivisme établis d'abord pendant le siècle des Lumières. Grâce à son instauration d'une série de publications, de colloques et de cours d'enseignement, ses idées et son œuvre se répandirent de l'activisme local jusqu'au domaine national et international. Il entraîna les artistes ainsi que les intellectuels dans son but d'améliorer les conditions de la vie physique et spirituelle. Selon lui la société était un tout organique qui évoluait à travers une 'loi de progrès'.

Ses méthodes réunissaient les dernières théories britanniques et françaises, reflétant l'intérêt particulier qu'il portait à Ruskin, Comte, Le Play et Taine. Ses activités à Edimbourg dans les années 1890 exprimaient une dynamique du moment et du lieu qu'on retrouve également chez Bergson et Durkheim.

Geddes traitait souvent du besoin de mémoire et d'entente collective culturelle. A Ramsay Garden, ensemble de constructions neuves et du dix-huitième siècle, il réanima, avec le soutien d'artistes et d'architectes locaux, le cœur de la géographie physique et intellectuel d'Edimbourg. Ses 'Summer Meetings of Science and Art' ainsi que les éditions de Patrick Geddes & Colleagues, notamment *The Evergreen* (1895-6), attiraient quelques uns des esprits les plus créateurs de France et d'Ecosse. La réunion qu'il organisa à Paris pendant toute la durée de l'Exposition Universelle de 1900 en fut la suite toute naturelle. La France fournissait la fondation institutionnelle et personnelle de son œuvre, dès l'instigation de la Société franco-écossaise dans les années 1890 jusqu'à son établissement d'un Collège des Ecossais à Montpellier lors de sa retraite à l'âge de soixante-dix ans.

II. *Artistic links between Scotland and France in the 1880s and 1890s*

FRANCES FOWLE

My starting point is the essay by James Paterson in the *Scottish Arts Review* of 1888 on 'Nationalism', in which he encourages Scots artists to be less parochial and look to France for their example. Many of the Glasgow Boys trained in Paris or spent time at Grez-sur-Loing; younger artists like Robert Brough travelled to Brittany and developed a style of painting strongly influenced by Gauguin and Sérusier. The International Exhibitions of 1886 (Edinburgh) and 1888 (Glasgow) had special Foreign Loan Sections for the display of French art, and dealers, especially in the 1890s, began specialising in French pictures – e.g. Alex Reid and his Société des Beaux-Arts. The influence on Scottish art of this period is clear, especially in the move towards a decorative, Symbolist style of painting in the late 1880s and 1890s.

In particular the essay focuses on artists such as E.A. Hornel, Robert Brough and John Duncan, all of whom worked in this new avant-garde style and contributed to Geddes's *Evergreen* review. It looks at the rise of mural painting and stained glass design in Glasgow in the 1880s and the concurrent interest in public decorative schemes in Paris. The importance of Japonisme and Japanese prints – brought over from Paris – to the development of Scottish art during this period is considered, as well as the developing fascination with the work of Puvis de Chavannes.

Relations artistiques entre l'Ecosse et la France entre 1880 et 1890

Le point de départ de cet essai est l'article sur le nationalisme écossais par James Paterson, publié dans le *Scottish Arts Review* en 1888. Dans cet article Paterson encourage les artistes écossais à abandonner leur esprit de clocher et à suivre l'exemple des artistes français. Bon nombre de 'Glasgow Boys' ont reçu leur formation dans des ateliers parisiens ou ont séjourné à Grez-sur-Loing; les plus jeunes artistes comme Robert Brough ont voyagé en Bretagne et ont développé un style de peinture influencé par Gauguin et Sérusier. Les Expositions Universelles de 1886 (à Edimbourg) et de 1888 (à Glasgow) ont eu des sections dediées à l'art français et hollandais, et les marchands écossais, surtout dans les années 90', se spécialisaient dans les tableaux français – par exemple, Alex Reid et sa galerie La Société des Beaux-Arts. L'influence de l'art français sur l'art écossais de cette période est remarquable, illustré par le développement des années 80' et 90' vers un style plus décoratif et symboliste.

En particulier, l'essai examine des artistes écossais comme E.A. Hornel, Robert Brough et John Duncan, qui ont developpé ce style avant-garde et qui ont contribué au *Evergreen*, le journal trimestriel de Patrick Geddes. La discussion se concentre sur la floraison de la peinture murale et du dessin des vitraux à cette époque à Glasgow, ainsi qu'à l'intérêt concurrent aux projets muraux dans les bâtiments publiques de Paris. Ce chapitre examine en plus l'importance de Pierre Puvis de Chavannes en Ecosse, ainsi que l'influence sur l'art écossais du japonisme et des estampes japonaises.

III. *Patrick Geddes's 'Clan d'Artistes': Some Elusive French Connections*

BELINDA THOMSON

The essay begins by exploring certain key aspects of Geddes's aesthetic tastes and cultural thinking, arguing that these owed much to his familiarity with the art and architecture of Third Republic France.

While Geddes's general commitment as a botanist/biologist to the idea of synergy can be seen translated into action in his schemes for the embellishment of Edinburgh and the animation of its cultural life, his specific concept of commissioning mural schemes for university halls and Ramsay Garden is related to contemporary decorative work by Puvis de Chavannes in Paris and Max Leenhardt in Montpellier.

A second section explores the close relations established in 1892-4 by the Edinburgh artist Charles Hodge Mackie with advanced painters in France – Paul Sérusier, Paul Ranson, Edouard Vuillard and Paul Gauguin – which led to a fascinating congruence with French styles in Mackie's work of the mid-1890s, particularly his decorative panels for Geddes's apartment and his cover design and illustrations for Geddes's journal, *The Evergreen*, 1895-6, to which Sérusier also contributed.

Thirdly, through the presence in Edinburgh of French anarchist writer Augustin Hamon, contacts were made between Geddes's circle and Lucien Pissarro, London-based printmaker and painter son of Camille Pissarro. The idea of mounting in Edinburgh an exhibition of advanced contemporary French painting was discussed.

In conclusion the essay considers why this period of intense cultural activity petered out after 1900 but points to Geddes's longer term successes in fostering Franco-Scottish cultural exchange. Geddes's decision to return to Montpellier at the end of his life and devote himself to the establishment of the Collège des Ecossais is seen as a logical reprise of his earlier endeavours in Scotland.

Le 'Clan d'Artistes' de Patrick Geddes: quelques liens français illusoires

Cet essai commence par prôner comme central au développement du goût esthétique et de la pensée culturelle de Geddes sa connaissance intime de l'art et de l'architecture français de la Troisième République.

Si, à la base de sa mise en œuvre de projets pour l'embellissement d'Edimbourg et pour l'animation de sa vie culturelle on trouve l'idée de synergie, à laquelle Geddes adhère en tant que botaniste et biologiste, sa vision et son idée de commander des ensembles décoratifs pour les résidences universitaires et pour son propre appartement à Ramsay Garden s'inspirent des ouvrages décoratifs contemporains de Puvis de Chavannes à Paris, et de Max Leenhardt, à Montpellier.

Une deuxième section examine les liens établis en 1892-4 entre Charles Hodge Mackie, artiste-peintre d'Edimbourg, et les Nabis, groupe de peintres d'avant-garde en France – Paul Sérusier, Paul Ranson, Edouard Vuillard et Paul Gauguin – liens qui expliquent le caractère incontestablement français de l'art de Mackie de l'époque.

En troisième lieu, grâce à la présence à Edimbourg d'Augustin Hamon, écrivain anarchiste, et de sa participation au cours d'enseignement de Geddes en 1895, un échange artistique s'établit entre le cercle de Geddes et Lucien Pissarro, fils aîné du peintre impressionniste et artiste graphique vivant à Londres. L'idée de monter une exposition de peinture contemporaine française à Edimbourg malheureusement ne porte pas fruit.

Pour conclure, l'essai considère les raisons pour lesquelles ce dynamisme culturel de Geddes ne se prolonge pas au-delà de 1900, et cite certains de ses succès à plus long terme. La décision de Geddes de s'établir à Montpellier à la fin de sa vie, pour s'y consacrer à l'établissement du Collège des Ecossais, peut être vu comme reprise logique de son activisme en Ecosse.

IV. *Patrick Geddes's French Connections in Academic and Political Life*
SIÂN REYNOLDS

This paper explores the various overlapping or discrete circles in France to which Patrick Geddes was connected in the years between 1878 and 1900. Following initial contacts with university scientists, met on his first field trips to Brittany, Geddes encountered other academics in Paris. He also met the sociological disciples of Frédéric Le Play and the positivists connected to Auguste Comte. A more surprising circle was that of the anarchist intellectuals. Through his interest in geography, Geddes initially encountered Kropotkin, then another anarchist geographer, Elisée Reclus. The Geddes and Reclus families remained connected by friendship and intermarriage. Many of these French academics and intellectuals gave lectures at the Edinburgh Summer Meetings in the 1890s. For the launch of the Franco-Scottish Society with Thomas Barclay in the 1890s, Geddes 'networked' the higher echelons of the French university system, and received support from politicians. In 1900, he drew on all his previous acquaintances, both for his ambitious summer school at the Paris International Exhibition, and in an unsuccessful bid to preserve its buildings as a series of museums. Although Geddes himself remained aloof from politics, analysis of the individuals in these different French circles shows that they shared a political position: support for the cause of Alfred Dreyfus during the Affair which shaped the political context of the1890s in France.

Les réseaux de Patrick Geddes en France

Ce chapitre analyse les cercles intellectuels auxquels Patrick Geddes s'associe en France entre 1878 et 1900. A partir de ses premiers contacts avec des scientifiques dans les années 1870, Geddes rencontre à Paris d'autres universitaires et surtout des disciples de F. Le Play et d'A. Comte, dont la pensée l'influencera. Son intérêt pour l'environnement l'approche cependant de certains géographes, tels P. Kropotkine et Elisée Reclus, anarchistes tous les deux. Les familles Geddes et Reclus s'uniront d'ailleurs par l'amitié et l'alliance. P. Geddes réussit à attirer dans ses 'Summer Meetings' à Edimbourg nombre d'universitaires ou intellectuels français pendant les années 1890. En 1895, il anime avec l'avocat écossais Thomas Barclay, installé à Paris, la Société Franco-Ecossaise, patronnée par les sommités de la Sorbonne entre autres. En 1900, il ravive tous ses réseaux français pour deux projets liés à l'Exposition de Paris: l'école internationale – sorte de cours universitaire d'été; et une tentative (qui échoue) de conserver les pavillons de l'Exposition en guise de musée permanent. Geddes lui-même se tiendra à l'écart de la vie politique, mais un fil réunit néanmoins la plupart de ses contacts français: le dreyfusisme.

V. *Patrick Geddes: from Edinburgh's Old Town to Paris's Exposition Universelle*

MURDO MACDONALD

Patrick Geddes was singled out in Edinburgh as 'the Scot who had best kept up the French connection'. In this light I explore Geddes's commitment to French art and ideas. In Edinburgh in the 1890s he encouraged contributions by French-speaking artists and writers (among them Paul Sérusier, Charles Sarolea, and Elisée Reclus) to his interdisciplinary magazine, *The Evergreen*. As a product of the Celtic revival in Scotland, *The Evergreen* published Celtic legends from Brittany in English-language versions. Reflections of the Auld Alliance between Scotland and France are clear in an illustration by John Duncan of Joan of Arc with her Scots Guards. Suggested by Andrew Lang, it was published in the *The Evergreen* to mark the opening of the Franco-Scottish Society at the Sorbonne in April 1896. Geddes had a deep respect for the international character of French culture and he saw the Universal Exhibition in Paris in 1900 as a means of furthering a global vision of cultural revival. To that end his contacts in Paris included not only his French friends, but the Hindu revivalist Swami Vivekananda and the Americal social reformer Jane Addams. In 1911 he gave further expression to France as his intellectual touchstone in his Masques of Learning. There he not only endorsed the Paris of Thomas Aquinas and Duns Scotus, but lamented that there was no longer a college to serve the needs of Scots students. Inspired by history to look to the future, he proposed the re-establishment of that Scots College.

Patrick Geddes : de la vieille ville d'Edimbourg à l'Exposition Universelle de Paris

Patrick Geddes fut identifié à Edimbourg comme 'L'Ecossais qui réussit le mieux à soutenir l'alliance française'. A ce titre j'examine l'adhérence de Geddes à l'art et aux idées français. A Edimbourg dans les années 1890 il sollicitait les contributions d'artistes et d'écrivains francophones (entre autres, Paul Sérusier, Charles Sarolea et Elisée Reclus) à son journal interdisciplinaire *The Evergreen*. Exemple de la Renaissance celtique en Ecosse, *The Evergreen* publia en version anglaise des légendes celtiques d'origine bretonne. Les souvenirs de *l'Auld Alliance* entre l'Ecosse et la France paraissent clairement dans l'illustration par John Duncan de Jeanne d'Arc et sa garde écossaise. Proposée par Andrew Lang, cette image fut publiée dans *The Evergreen* pour fêter l'inauguration de la Société franco-écossaise à la Sorbonne en avril 1896. Geddes avait beaucoup de respect pour le caractère international de la culture française et pour lui l'Exposition Universelle de 1900 à Paris paraissait comme moyen d'avancer une vision globale de renaissance culturelle. Ainsi son réseau de contacts à Paris comportait non seulement des amis français, mais le revivaliste hindu Swami Vivekenanda et la réformatrice sociale américaine, Jane Addams. En 1911 dans ses 'Masques of Learning' il exprima une nouvelle fois à quel point la France lui servait d'inspiration intellectuelle. Non seulement y soutenait-il le Paris de Thomas d'Aquin et de Duns Scotus, mais il regretta la disparition du Collège des Ecossais pour répondre aux besoins des étudiants écossais. Inspiré par l'histoire à se tourner vers l'avenir, il proposa le rétablissement de ce même Collège des Ecossais.

Select Bibliography

Armour, Margaret, 'Mural decoration in Scotland, Part I', *The Studio*, Vol.10, Feb. 1897, pp.100-6

Boardman, Philip, *Esquisse de l'oeuvre éducatrice de Patrick Geddes*, Montpellier 1936

Boardman, Philip, *Patrick Geddes: Maker of the Future*, Chapel Hill 1944

Boardman, Philip, *The Worlds of Patrick Geddes: Biologist, Town Planner, Re-educator, Peace-Warrior*, London 1978

Bowe, Nicola Gordon & Cumming, Elizabeth, *The Arts and Crafts Movements in Dublin and Edinburgh 1885-1925*, Dublin 1998

Caw, James L., *Scottish Painting Past and Present, 1620-1908*, Edinburgh 1908

Cumming, Elizabeth, *Arts and Crafts in Edinburgh 1880-1930*, Edinburgh 1985

Defries, Amelia, *The Interpreter: Geddes, the Man and his Gospel*, London 1927

The Evergreen: A Northern Seasonal. The Book of Spring, Patrick Geddes & Colleagues, Edinburgh and T. Fisher Unwin, London 1895

The Evergreen: A Northern Seasonal. The Book of Autumn, Patrick Geddes & Colleagues, Edinburgh, T. Fisher Unwin, London and J.B. Lippincott Co., Philadelphia 1895

The Evergreen: A Northern Seasonal.The Book of Summer, Patrick Geddes & Colleagues, Edinburgh, T. Fisher Unwin, London and J.B. Lippincott Co., Philadelphia 1896

The Evergreen: A Northern Seasonal. The Book of Winter, Patrick Geddes & Colleagues, Edinburgh, T. Fisher Unwin, London and J.B. Lippincott Co., Philadelphia 1896-7

Fraser, Bashabi (ed.), *Geddes Tagore Correspondence*, Edinburgh 2002

Geddes, Anna, 'Montpellier and its ancient university', *The (Scottish) Art Review*, Jan.-June 1890, pp.130-4

Geddes, Patrick & Thomson, J. Arthur, *The Evolution of Sex*, London 1889

Geddes, Patrick & Thomson, J. Arthur, *Evolution*, London & New York 1911

Geddes, Patrick, *Cities in Evolution: An Introduction to the Town Planning Movement and to the Study of Civics*, London 1915

Hardie, William, *Scottish Painting, 1837 to the Present*, London 1990

The Interpreter: Of Seven Pictures. Of Black and White, Patrick Geddes & Colleagues, Edinburgh, April 1896

Kitchen, Paddy, *A Most Unsettling Person: The Life and Ideas of Patrick Geddes, Founding Father of City Planning and Environmentalism*, New York 1975

Macdonald, Murdo, 'Patrick Geddes and Charles Rennie Mackintosh',
    Newsletter of the Charles Rennie Mackintosh Society, No.76, Summer
    1999, p.12

Macdonald, Murdo, 'The Patron, the Professor and the Painter: cultural
    activity in Dundee at the close of the nineteenth century', in Louise
    Mitchell, Christopher A. Whatley, Bob Harris (eds), *Victorian Dundee:
    Image and Realities*, East Linton 2000, pp.135-50

Macmillan, Duncan, *Scottish Art 1460-1990*, Edinburgh 1990

Mavor, James, *My Windows on the Street of the World*, 2 Vols, London &
    New York 1923

Meller, Helen, *Patrick Geddes: Social Evolutionist and City Planner*, London
    1990 (paperback edn 1993)

Robertson, Pamela (ed.), *Charles Rennie Mackintosh: The Architectural
    Papers*, Wendlebury 1990

Robertson, Stewart, *A Moray Loon*, Edinburgh 1933

*Transactions of the National Association for the Advancement of Art and its
    Application to Industry, Edinburgh Meeting, MDCCCLXXXIX*, London
    1890

Welter, Volker, *Biopolis: Patrick Geddes and the City of Life*, Cambridge
    Mass. 2002

Willsdon, Clare, 'Paul Sérusier the Celt; did he paint murals in Edin-
    burgh?' *Burlington Magazine*, Vol.126, No.971, Feb. 1984, pp.88-91

Willsdon, Clare, *Mural Painting in Britain, 1840-1940. Image and Mean-
    ing*, Oxford 2000

Index